Grant Cooper
Artistic Director and Conductor | ORCHESTRA

P.O. Box 2292 • Charleston, WV 25328

2017 Vaughan Fellowship

Piper McLaughlin

THE LITTLE RED BOOK OF

MUSICIANS' WISDOM

THE LITTLE RED BOOK OF
MUSICIANS' WISDOM

Sheila E. Anderson

Skyhorse Publishing

All Rights Reserved. No part of this book may be reproduced in any manner without the express written consent of the publisher, except in the case of brief excerpts in critical reviews or articles. All inquiries should be addressed to Skyhorse Publishing, 307 West 36th Street, 11th Floor, New York, NY 10018.

Skyhorse Publishing books may be purchased in bulk at special discounts for sales promotion, corporate gifts, fund-raising, or educational purposes. Special editions can also be created to specifications. For details, contact the Special Sales Department, Skyhorse Publishing, 307 West 36th Street, 11th Floor, New York, NY 10018 or info@skyhorsepublishing.com.

Skyhorse® and Skyhorse Publishing® are registered trademarks of Skyhorse Publishing, Inc.®, a Delaware corporation.

Visit our website at www.skyhorsepublishing.com.

10 9 8 7 6 5 4 3 2 1

Library of Congress Cataloging-in-Publication Data is available on file.
ISBN: 978-1-61608-855-2

Printed in China

To my brother Arthur Sayres Anderson Jr., "Chips," who passed away in 1976 at the age of twenty-six. It was he who encouraged my love of music. He gave me my name and many life lessons. To him I will always be grateful!

Contents

Acknowledgments

This book could not have come to be had it not been for Tony Lyons, who took seriously my one-page, three-paragraph proposal for a book to be titled *The Quotable Jazz Lover*. My timing was perfect, because Tony had a "publisher friend" who was looking for someone to write a quotable book about *all* music. When I had the initial brainstorm, it was Steve Bedney who encouraged me to propose my idea to Tony Lyons and Lisa Purcell, who then sent me to a Web site dedicated to quotes. Without Richard Rothschild, I could never have written the proposal in the first place. Richard not only guided me through the proposal process, but he also walked me through the contract and my first draft.

Once I got over the shock that I was going to write this book, my friend Eric Reed loaded me up with quotable and music books from his library. He gave me information as well as invaluable criticism as I began to amass quotes (though he liked very few). My dear Jeff Clayton not only gave me wonderful quotes, original and otherwise, but he also kept me laughing and on track when I began to get off.

I must also thank the very busy Randall Kenan for reading my first draft in record time. He continues to be a source of inspiration and joy for me, after all these years of friendship. Thanks to Tina Marshall, who became an unofficial research assistant as she surfed the Internet to find quotes and other last-minute information.

I could not have compiled such great words without the help of the following people, who readily shared their quotes with me: James Browne (the first to ever give me quotable material), Kevin Powell, Charlie Braxton, Michael Bourne, Gary Walker, Bob Porter, Felix Hernandez, Awilda Rivera, Ira Gitler, Lou Donaldson, Dr. Lonnie Smith, Harry Allen, Bobby Sanabria, Bill Charlap, Javon Jackson, Russell Malone, Duduka Da Fonseca, Peter Leitch, John Hicks, Kenny Barron, Benny Green, Gene Davis, Mike LeDonne, Ira Nepus, David Hazeltine, Cedar Walton, Joel Katz, Bob Stewart, Kenny Washington, Todd Elder, and Eric Rucker. I also wish to thank Tad Crawford, who took a chance on me, and Nicole Potter, who was so patient throughout this process. Thanks to Kate Lothman for her thoughtful and sensitive editing, to Liz Van Hoose for her hard work, and to everyone else who had a hand on my manuscript.

To my other friends who encouraged me along the way: Pat and Allan Harris (they fed me, too), Ellen Cash (who would bring me dinner from Carmine's on Friday evenings), Megan Van Peebles, Francesca B. Mesiah, Harvey S. Wise (who helped me continue my jazz education), my colleagues at The Newark Museum, Linda Nettleton (who kept me calm and directed), Lucy Brotman (who never complained about my hours), Ward Mintz (who is so cool), Mary Sue Sweeney Price, and Pat Faison. To Thurston Briscoe (who did not make me feel guilty for taking off from *Sunday Morning Harmony* to finish the book), and to Aaron Richman, Lottie Gooding, Linda Prather, Nancy Cristy, and all of my publishing friends who are too numerous to name. Of course,

Acknowledgments

I give my love, respect, and admiration to my mom Estelle, my dad Arthur, my sister Michele, and my brother Michael. They were my first influences.

I'd like to thank the sources of some favorite quotes of mine (which do not come from musicians at all). One of my publishing friends, Denny Ortman, told me that after he had quit smoking, a bum on the street asked him for a cigarette. Proud of having quit, Denny said, "I quit!" The bum responded, "What did you quit for? You're gonna die anyway!" Another favorite quote came from my father. He asked a man with a drinking problem how he had become a drunk. The man's response: "Hey, Art, when is the last time anyone said to you, 'have a sandwich on me!'?" My all-time favorite is a quote from my mother, one I use often: "Fake it 'til you make it!"

B.S.: Wow! It takes all types to make the world go 'round.

Introduction

As a child growing up in Buffalo, New York, music was my refuge. By night, I slept with the radio at my ear, and by day, I occupied the only record player in the house when my siblings allowed me access. Music was a constant in our household, and we all had our individual tastes. Chips, my oldest brother, listened to almost everything, though he preferred traditional jazz and blues and The Beatles; my sister Michele liked rock; my brother Michael listened to Motown and R&B, as did I, mostly. However, when I was allowed, I would listen to my two favorite albums of Chips's: Miles Davis's *E.S.P.* and Richard "Groove" Holmes's *Soul Message*. On Sunday, my mother made us turn off our music. Sunday was *her* day to listen to what *she* wanted to hear, which was classical, folk, Duke Ellington, and Mahalia Jackson.

As a teenager, at parties, I took charge of the turntable and became the unofficial disc jockey. I would sit for hours listening to music and reading the back of album covers, and when the technology became available (to Chips's horror), I made tapes of my favorite songs. Chips taught me at a young age how to respect music and how to listen to it. He was very possessive of his albums, so he instructed me on how to hold them. If he witnessed me putting my fingers on the albums or stacking the 45s on the turntable he would yell at me, give me a lecture—or, worse, not allow me to listen to them at all.

Music Is a Measure of Popular Culture

While I was a teenager and young adult, popular music evolved by leaps and bounds, and its cultural significance became all the more apparent. When The Beatles landed in America, I remember the controversy the band caused by being so outspoken (and for wearing long hair). The 1960s was a decade of change, and music reflected this: Motown came to be; rock and folk music evolved; and, as the Vietnam War raged on, so did the protest songs. Those were turbulent and exciting times; I remember listening to Joan Baez, Joni Mitchell, Marvin Gaye, James Taylor, Carole King, Miles Davis, Count Basie, The Rolling Stones, Ike and Tina Turner, and countless other musicians who dared to be different and make a statement, personally and musically.

During the 1970s, black Americans were feeling a sense of pride, as reflected in James Brown's song "Say it Loud: I'm Black and I'm Proud." Women were also fighting for equality amidst all the talk about peace and the songs about love. Crosby, Stills, Nash, and Young perhaps summed up the spirit of the decade best with the anthem, "Love the One You're With." Donna Summer rang in the disco era with "Love to Love You Baby," while Marvin Gaye crooned "Sexual Healing."

In 1980, Michael Jackson's "Billie Jean," and the rift MTV caused when it decided not to show the video, fell victim to the controversy that would characterize much of popular music throughout the upcoming decades. It is this distinctive controversy that speaks volumes about the nature of music, its effect on its listeners, and its encapsulation of popular culture.

The Human Behind the Musician

As I examine how music has shaped my perception of my life, I see that my constant love of music has been shaped, above all, by my constant love of people. As I compiled this book, I felt that the musicians were talking *to me*. Indeed, I have a much better understanding of the musician now that I have discovered such a wide range of quotes and examined music through the musicians' own eyes.

Working on *The Little Red Book of Musician's Wisdom* has been exciting and rewarding. When I embarked on this project, I was worried that I would not find enough material. However, I quickly saw that I had nothing to worry about; in fact, there was an abundance of material. As I sifted through the piles of magazines and books in my apartment, I was amazed at what I found. For the first time, I was thankful that I am such a pack rat—I found magazines that dated back to the early 1980s. As I rifled through the material, it brought back many vivid memories: going to parties with friends; trying to sing all of the words to the Queen song "Bohemian Rhapsody"; studying my flute and attempting both to transcribe one of Bach's Brandenburg Concertos and to play Eric Dolphy's daunting solo on "Left Alone"; and searching on Saturday nights, during my days as a disco diva, for the perfect hustle dance partner.

It was my intent, when I was asked to produce a book of quotes, that the collection also reflect my personality as well as the characters of the people whose words I have collected. I consider myself to be an intelligent observer, a cynic, an introvert who can be an extrovert, a contemplative, and someone who can at times be so silly that I make myself, and others, laugh. These qualities are what have instilled in me a love of so many different genres

Introduction

of music. It is my hope that you'll find glimpses into the distinct and various personalities of the musicians and others quoted in this book—which I hope might make their words all the more powerful.

These quotes are compiled from many sources—books, magazines, the Internet, documentaries, and people who shared their own quotes that were either original or given to them by musicians. In a way, this book wrote itself. What has come of this endeavor is more than I expected. Instead of being simply a book of quotes, it is a study of music and its makers. As you read through these pages, you will see the connections between all kinds of music, throughout the ages. You will read quotes from jazz musicians and rappers who talk of being influenced by classical musicians. You will read about how similarly many musicians view society, how they feel about their art, and how they infuse their lives with humor to overcome the challenges musicianship can bring. You'll find that the classical musicians were as critical of each other, and of critics, as musicians are today. They were also as flawed, fragile, funny, and introspective as modern-day musicians.

At times, the quotes in this book seem to make the musicians come alive; they are not just words on a page. *The Little Red Book of Musician's Wisdom* is a book of quotes from Bach to Tupac. It is a glimpse into their music and into the people they are, and it shows how blessed we are that they have added something special to this planet. Perhaps you will do as I have done: read the book, listen to their music, and feel better for having done so.

CHAPTER 1

On the Definition of Music

Music is the shorthand of emotion.
—Leo Tolstoy

• • •

True music must repeat the thought and inspirations of the people and the time.
My people are Americans and my time is today.
—George Gershwin

• • •

It don't mean a thing if it ain't got that swing.
—Duke Ellington (and Irving Mills)

• • •

On the Definition of Music

Jazz is an art, not a subjective phenomenon.
—STANLEY CROUCH

• • •

Extraordinary how potent cheap music is . . .
—NOEL COWARD

• • •

These days, there is more rhythm in our lives than harmony.
—JEFF CLAYTON, TO WAYNE SHORTER

• • •

No two people on earth are alike, and it's got to be that way in music, or it isn't music.
—BILLIE HOLIDAY

• • •

All music is folk music, I ain't never heard no horse sing a song.
—LOUIS ARMSTRONG

• • •

I think if it wasn't for the blues, there wouldn't be no jazz.
—T-BONE WALKER

• • •

Music is the divine way to tell beautiful, poetic things to the heart.
—PABLO CASALS

• • •

Without music, life would be an error.
The German imagines even God singing songs.
—FRIEDRICH NIETZSCHE

• • •

Music is your own experience, your own thoughts, your wisdom.
If you don't live it, it won't come out of your horn.
They teach you there's no boundary line to music.
But, man, there's no boundary line in art.
—CHARLIE PARKER

• • •

Music hath charms to soothe the savage breast, to soften rocks, or
bend a troubled oak.
—WILLIAM CONGREVE

• • •

Music is the soul of language.
—MAX HEINDEL

• • •

Every mistake is a new style.
—ALHAJI IBRAHIM ABDULAI, A DRUMMER FROM NORTH
GHANA, AS TOLD BY ERIC RUCKER

• • •

The music is not part of this planet in a sense that the spirit of it is about happiness. Most musicians play earth things about what they know, but I found out that they are mostly unhappy and frustrated, and that creeps over into their music.
—Sun Ra

• • •

Music is moonlight in the gloomy night of life.
—Jean Paul Richter

• • •

The mastership in music and in life, in fact, is not something that can be taught—it can only be caught.
—Rodney Jones, jazz guitarist

• • •

CHAPTER 2

On Identity

Only become a musician if there is absolutely no other way you can make a living.
—Kirke Mecham

• • •

Being a singer, a writer, an actress, and whatever else that I choose to do is not all that I am. . . . I am a woman. I make mistakes. I make them often. . . . God has given me a talent.
—Jill Scott

• • •

On Identity

I am not a blues singer. I am not a jazz singer. I am not a country singer. But I am a singer who can sing the blues, who can sing jazz, who can sing country.
—RAY CHARLES

• • •

No one understands another's grief, no one understands another's joy. . . . My music is the product of my talent and my misery. And that which I have written in my greatest distress is what the world seems to like best.
—FRANZ SCHUBERT

• • •

Soul was always here, but the form of arrangement, what we called soul, changed with me, because I took jazz and gospel and made it funk, and we started dealin' with it a little different.
—JAMES BROWN, TO FELIX HERNANDEZ, HOST OF *THE RHYTHM REVIEW* ON JAZZ 88.3 FM, WBGO, NEWARK

• • •

I'm three in one: Fats Waller, Louis Armstrong, and a fellow by the name of Gatemouth Moore. You'll hear all three of us when I sing. Out of the three I developed my own style.
—RUFUS THOMAS, TO FELIX HERNANDEZ, HOST OF *THE RHYTHM REVIEW* ON JAZZ 88.3 FM, WBGO, NEWARK

• • •

I've always been a musician, and I've always tried to keep developing new ideas. . . . Since I see change as a natural process, I think I've always been changing and developing my music. It's hard for me to state precisely which directions I took, but I have moved along using my feelings and intuition. I have always looked to pop, reggae, and jazz for ideas since the beginning of my musical career, but through the years I have substantially incorporated them more and more into my owe musical expression.
—GILBERTO GIL

• • •

If the music is eccentric, I have to be. Anybody talented in any way—they're called eccentric.
—THELONIOUS MONK

• • •

I'll be your trick and your treat!
—JOHNNY GARRY COMMENTING ABOUT BEING BORN ON HALLOWEEN

• • •

No, I always thought of myself as a painter in show business [laughs]. How did I end up here? I never identified myself for years, really, even as a musician. I just thought of myself as a painter who played. But I did have a compositional gift. And I've been at it so long that I have a certain amount of identity as a musician.
—JONI MITCHELL

• • •

On Identity

My love was rock and the blues.
I put the *swing* into the blues,
I made the blues JUMP!
I wasn't tryin' to change the style.
I was just trying to give it life.
—Joe Turner, to Felix Hernandez, host of *THE
RHYTHM REVIEW* on Jazz 88.3 FM, WBGO, Newark

• • •

Isn't the artist's real job to learn from nature? Instead of churning
out pop hits, shouldn't the truly talented among us be listening to
the flutter of a butterfly's wing?
—Marvin Gaye

• • •

It was called the Backstreet Market, and it was just like a local
hangout. That was where the kids would drive their cars, hang
out with their convertibles, and listen to music. That's how we got
"Backstreet." We put "Boys" on it, because no matter how old we
get, we'll always be boys.
—Kevin Richardson

• • •

Learning to read music in Braille and play by ear helped me
develop a damn good memory.
—Ray Charles

• • •

On Identity

We are the music makers, and we are the dreamers of the dream.
Wandering by lone sea breakers, and sitting by desolate streams.
World losers and world forsakers, for whom the pale moon
gleams. Yet we are movers and the shakers of the world forever
it seems.
—ARTHUR O'SHAUNESSEY

• • •

We called ourselves the Warlocks and we found out that some
other band already had that name. . . . I picked up a dictionary
and literally the first thing I saw when I looked down on a page
was The Grateful Dead. It was a little creepy, but I thought it was
a striking combination of words.
—JERRY GARCIA

• • •

We never play anything the same way once.
—SHELLY MANNE

• • •

Folk music is where I live. Folk music straightened my back and
it kinked my hair. What is an Afro or natural today used to be
called an Odetta.
—ODETTA

• • •

You can separate the men from the boys and ballads.
—COLEMAN HAWKINS, SAXOPHONIST

CHAPTER 3

• • •

On Composing

My main goal is to tell a story.
—STEPHEN SONDHEIM

• • •

I don't like composers who think. It gets in the way of their
plagiarism.
—HOWARD DIETZ

• • •

The secret of writing a good popular song is to make it melodi-
cally simple and harmonically attractive.
—JULE STYNE, TO BILL CHARLAP, PIANIST

• • •

BARRON: How are you doing?
HICKS: I'm writing some music.
BARRON: How's it going?
HICKS: Four liars at a time.
A conversation between pianists Kenny Barron and John Hicks

• • •

I have learned throughout my life as a composer chiefly through my mistakes and pursuits of false assumptions, not by my exposure to wisdom and founts of knowledge.
—IGOR STRAVINSKY

• • •

HAMMERSTEIN: Here is a story laid in China about an Italian told by an Irishman. What kind of music are you going to write?
KERN: It'll be good Jewish music.
Jerome Kern in the 1930s, discussing with Oscar Hammerstein II a musical to be based on Brian Oswald Bonn-Byrne's novel Messer Marco Polo

• • •

I wish I could write librettos for the rest of my life. It is the purest of human pleasures, a heavenly hermaphroditism of being both writer and musician. No wonder that selfish beast Wagner kept it to himself.
—SYLVIA TOWNSEND WARNER

• • •

William "Count" Basie was the man who turned the Neal Hefti tune "Lil' Darlin,'" originally a medium tempo, into a ballad and made it a jazz standard. Without a doubt, Count Basie was the indisputable leader of swing, the man who was responsible for swinging the blues. The "Count" is King.
—SHEILA ANDERSON

• • •

If a young man at the age of twenty-three can write a symphony like that, in five years he will be ready to commit murder.
—WALTER DAMROSCH, ON AARON COPLAND

• • •

A good composer is slowly discovered; a bad composer is slowly found out.
—ERNEST NEWMAN

• • •

A good composer does not imitate, he steals.
—IGOR STRAVINSKY

• • •

People never write pretty melodies for tubas. It just isn't done.
—GEORGE KLEINSINGER AND PAUL TRIPP

• • •

On Composing

Give me a laundry list and I'll set it to music.
—GIOACCHINO A. ROSSINI

• • •

It's a marvelous feeling when someone says, "I want to do
this song of yours," because they've connected to it.
That's what I'm after.
—MARY CHAPIN CARPENTER

• • •

Composition is notation of distortion of what composers think
they've heard before. Masterpieces are marvelous misquotations.
—NED ROREM

• • •

He understood the violin as well as he understood jazz, and he
wrote for the violin as a violin.
—STEPHANE GRAPPELLI, ON BILLY STRAYHORN

• • •

I pick the tune, you know, just on the strings. That's the way I did
all my songs. I reckon that's why they named it "cotton pickin.' "
—ELIZABETH COTTON, GRAMMY WINNER IN 1984 AND
AUTHOR OF THE FOLK CLASSIC "FREIGHT TRAIN"

• • •

On Composing

The way to write American music is simple. All you have to do is be an American and then write any kind of music you wish.
—VIRGIL THOMPSON

• • •

I once sent him a song and asked him to mark a cross wherever he thought it was faulty. Brahms returned it untouched, saying, "I don't want to make a cemetery of your composition."
—HUGO WOLF

• • •

I never asked how.
—WOLFGANG AMADEUS MOZART, AS RECOUNTED BY ISAAC ASIMOV
A young, would-be composer wrote to Mozart, asking advice as to how to compose a symphony. Mozart responded that a symphony was a complex and demanding musical form and that it would be better to start with something simpler. "But Herr Mozart," the young man protested, "you wrote symphonies when you were younger than I am now."

• • •

There are still so many beautiful things to be said in C Major.
—SERGEI PROKOFIEV

• • •

It is clear that the first specification for a composer is to be dead.
—ARTHUR HONEGGER

• • •

The first professional pop song I ever wrote was called "Could It Be Magic?" which I based on Chopin's Prelude in C Minor. The song came in at eight minutes. I didn't know that I wasn't supposed to write a song that was over two minutes long. That's how out of touch with pop music I was. I still am.

—Barry Manilow

• • •

Now the idea that the melody must always be in the upper voice and that the constant collaboration of the other voices is a fault is one for which I have been able to find no sufficient grounds. Rather it is the exact opposite that flows from the nature of music. For music consists of harmony, and harmony becomes far more complete if all the voices collaborate to form it.

—Johann Sebastian Bach

• • •

What I think makes the difference . . . , I know as for me and the rest of the Pound . . . is that we always try to keep our music bass-heavy. . . . When it comes to us, it's less music, all drums. I keep my music simple. The simpler it is, the easier it is for you to mix it. Once you get the beat . . . the beat is the heart of the song, period, regardless to how you put it. The music is gonna groove you, but the beat is what makes you move.

—KLC, producer for the Medicine Men (formerly known as Beats by the Pounds), to Charlie Braxton, music journalist and cultural critic

• • •

CHAPTER 4

On the Effects of Music

The effects of good music are not just because it's new; on the contrary, music strikes us more the more familiar we are with it.
—Johann Wolfgang von Goethe

• • •

Life can't be all bad when for $10 you can buy all the Beethoven sonatas and listen to them for ten years.
—William F. Buckley, Jr.

• • •

Music was my refuge. I could crawl into the space between the notes and curl my back to loneliness.
—Maya Angelou

• • •

The flute is not an instrument with a good moral effect. It is too exciting.
—ARISTOTLE

• • •

How can one express the indefinable sensations that one experiences while writing an instrumental composition that has no definite subject? It is a purely lyrical process. It is a musical confession of the soul, which unburdens itself through sounds, just as a lyric poet expresses himself through poetry. . . . As the poet Heine said, "Where words leave off, music begins."
—PIOTR ILYICH TCHAIKOVSKY

• • •

You can't possibly hear the last movement of Beethoven's Seventh and go slow.
—OSCAR LEVANT, EXPLAINING HIS WAY OUT OF A SPEEDING TICKET

• • •

Music is the key to a female's heart.
—JOHANN G. SEUME

• • •

My idea is that there is music in the air, music all around us, the world is full of it, and you simply take as much as you require.
—SIR EDWARD ELGAR

• • •

I am the son of two Baptist ministers. My mother and father were both ministers. For me, faith was a double-edged sword, because it was both a choice as well as an obligation. The musical aspect as well as the soul and the gospel were something I could always feel because it was so uplifting. I loved the way that gospel music made me feel.

—CEE-LO GREEN TO CHARLIE BRAXTON, MUSIC JOURNALIST AND CULTURAL CRITIC

• • •

One good thing about music: When it hits you, you feel no pain.
—T. J. CHRISTOFORE

• • •

The music in my heart I bore. Long after it was heard no more.
—WILLIAM WORDSWORTH

• • •

There is no feeling, except the extremes of fear and grief that does not find relief in music.
—GEORGE ELIOT

• • •

On the Effects of Music

It's not that we might get the audience excited, we can't help it—
because this is the most highly engineered and exciting music
that has ever been and will ever be created.
—Eddie Palmieri, pianist and bandleader, referring
to Afro-Cuban music, as told by Bobby Sanabria,
percussionist

• • •

Ouch!
—Grover Washington, Jr.
*Washington said this under his breath when he heard something
that he liked as a judge in the Hennessy jazz search. As told by
Michael Bourne, Weekday Afternoon and* Singers Unlimited *host
on Jazz 88.3 FM, WBGO, Newark, who had also been a judge.*

• • •

When I used to watch my mother sing, which was usually in
church, that feeling, that soul, that thing—it's like electricity
rolling through you—that's what I wanted. When I watched
Aretha sing . . . the way she closed her eyes, and that riveting
thing just came out. People just . . . *oooh*, it could stop you in
your tracks.
—Whitney Houston

• • •

Sweet . . . sweet!
—Benny Green, pianist, upon hearing something that
he likes very much

• • •

CHAPTER 5

On Being Ron Carter

Ron Carter has been a world-class bassist and cellist since the 1960s. He's among the greatest accompanists of all time, but he has also done many solo albums exhibiting his prodigious technique. Carter is nearly as accomplished in classical music as in jazz and has performed with symphony orchestras all over the world. He played in the Eastman School of Music Philharmonic Orchestra and gained his degree from the school in 1959. He moved to New York City and played In Chico Hamilton's quintet with Eric Dolphy while also enrolled at the Manhattan School of Music, where he earned his master's degree in 1961. He worked with Randy Weston and Thelonious Monk and played and recorded with Jaki Byard in the early 1960s.

Carter joined Art Farmer's group for a short time in 1963, before he was tapped to become a member of Miles Davis's band.

He remained with Davis until 1968, appearing on every crucial mid-1960s recording and teaming with Herbie Hancock and Tony Williams to craft a new, freer rhythm-section sound. He is possibly the most recorded bassist in jazz history. He's led his own bands, at various intervals, since 1972.

As a band leader he has recorded more than fifty albums. Carter also contributed many arrangements and compositions to both his groups and other bands. He even invented his own instrument: a piccolo bass. His recordings have encompassed an unusually imaginative range of Ideas—from cello ensembles to reexaminations of Bach. At the age of sixty-six, Ron Carter has become an elder statesman of jazz. He continues to share his time, his talent, and his knowledge with younger musicians. He is an elegant, proud, erudite, private man with a great sense of humor, who gives generously to those he calls friends, The following quotes are words spoken by Ron to other musicians, as well as excerpts from my 1999 Interview with him for my TV program *The Art of Jazz* on Time Warner Cable's Manhattan Neighborhood Network. He was quite candid about his views on critics, other musical forms, and his role as a bass player.

• • •

Some drummers think time is only a magazine.
—As Told By Bobby Sanabria, Percussionist

• • •

Producer-manager James Browne, owner of the club Sweet Rhythm, had been in London for an emcee job. A promoter wanted Browne to call Ron Carter and ask him if he would come to London to play a gig. Browne, not wanting to make the call knowing that the fee would probably be inadequate, finally called Carter and told him that the promoter wanted him to come to London with his group to perform. When Carter asked Browne how much the fee was, he told him $2,000. Carter's response: "Is that $2,000 per note?"

● ● ●

Is there another level that you can set your guitar to, other than stun?

—To guitarist Russell Malone, at pianist Benny Green's date at the Village Vanguard in 1997
Carter thought that Malone had played a little loud.
(Other members of the band were Lewis Nash and Antonio Hart.)

● ● ●

Then why don't you call me and get me off of your list?

—To Guitarist Russell Malone
Upon their meeting, a nervous Malone told Carter that he was one of the many musicians whom he had on his list of people to play with.

● ● ●

ANDERSON: There are so many definitions of jazz. Do you have a definition, or do you think that people are trying to categorize it in too many ways?

CARTER: I think that the categorization that people are determined to have, it really isn't necessary to enjoy whatever your view of the music is. I don't hear of anyone going to the New York Philharmonic and standing outside saying, "And what's the definition of classical music? What's the definition of Mozart's music?" They just go and enjoy the music. I think that we have allowed the critics to determine how we view a definition, as it makes the music more important than it is to us. My own way to give you a definition is to give you some examples of people to go to hear, not make recommendations. . . . I avoid getting involved in specific definitions.

● ● ●

ANDERSON: What is it, specifically, with the bass—what is it that I should listen for? The bass in relationship to the drums, or on its own?

CARTER: My view is that the bass player, whoever he or she happens to be, is actually the quarterback of the band. That's to say, the bass player wishes a certain part of a tune to be louder or softer in volume, or they want the sound to be half as fast as the previous section was. The bass player controls those kinds of musical dynamics. He will play certain kind of notes that will catch the soloist's attention or the band's attention, or he will play a phrase that startles everybody in the band. Those are things that you can see—that will let you know that the bass player is not only involved in the band, but he has affected the band for those few moments. . . . If you see this happen, what you are seeing is a rare event, not only in that you see the musician try to affect a band's musical thoughts, process, and progress, but in that the band has heard that and is responding to it.

• • •

ANDERSON: As my listening improves, as I hear a song and see musicians and how they interact, should I assume that if people on the bandstand look like they are having a good time, that something has happened?

CARTER: By and large, that's a good view, but I have to use these imperative examples to show you in the process what has happened to jazz. When you go to the ballet, no one is sitting next to you explaining to you what the dancers are doing. . . . [One] goes to the ballet *Swan Lake*, they see the performance, and everyone leaves happy. But they are just as musically ignorant as to what it took to make the performance work as when they walked in. . . . But when one goes to a jazz club, everyone has to be a jazz historian on any instrument or the music to be able to understand what went on, because they are putting these different criteria for musical definitions and what you expect to know about the music and its performers before or after you leave. It tends to make the listening pleasure smaller.

• • •

ANDERSON: Was it always this way?

CARTER: Earlier critics said music was great if one needed an opinion. By and large, we've become more critic-trusting. . . . If a movie gets one star, automatically ticket sales drop off without people going to see it. Same with a jazz club. . . . We've entrusted them with way too much influence on some of the choices we make. Years ago that was not the case.

• • •

ANDERSON: You seem to be able to anticipate what is coming up.
CARTER: I'm always thinking ahead of the tune. . . . That is one of the things I enjoy doing, but you can't do it unless you know the song.

• • •

ANDERSON: You write songs. Do you write lyrics as well?
CARTERS: No.

• • •

ANDERSON: You made recordings of classical music with jazz influences—is that a proper description? I happen to like how yon handled the material.

CARTER: Well, you know, they are trying to play the same twelve notes I'm trying to play. If those people who are so steeped in the classical tradition are unable to accept anyone else's view of a classical piece but theirs, then, they are really missing out on what music is all about. Just to play a game, I would defy those people to sit in a chair and listen to fifteen versions of Beethoven's Fifth and tell me which is better and why, because they will not all sound the same. But they become offended when a jazz musician adds a high hat to a Bartok piece.

• • •

ANDERSON: You played on three thousand albums (and that is probably on the low side)... How was it to adjust to the Brazilian form?

CARTER: Not really knowing the music, when Carlos Jobim came to New York [City], it was his second U.S. record made in the U.S. playing with his band, playing his music. I was aware of Dizzy [Gillespie] playing his music, and I was aware of the Stan Getz and Charlie Byrd record, but I never spent time to learn what it really did. . . . I just didn't have time to see what was going on and to be part of the music. . . . I knew who he [Jobim] was, and I had seen the movie *Black Orpheus* . . . so I was aware of the emotional impact that it had, but I never spent time to say, what really *is* that?

[Playing Brazilian] was like playing bebop. It used the same kind of harmonic basis for the songs. My view of the bass player's job is always to play what you can to maintain the person's view of the music who hires you but have enough left of your own personal input so that it does not sound like a job that anyone else can do. . . . Fortunately, I picked the right notes, [I] picked the right rhythms. . . . *Wave* and *Storm,* they were some wonderful Brazilian records.

• • •

CHAPTER 6

On Performing and Rehearsing

I never understood the need for a "live" audience. My music, because of its extreme quietude, would be happiest with a dead one.

—IGOR STRAVINSKY

• • •

I would like to play for audiences who are not using my music to stimulate their sex organs.

—ORNETTE COLEMAN

• • •

I work 865 days a year, because my mind never quits on me. The one-nighters is one way of gettin' rid of energy, but I do it now with my head. Mentally, it's the same thing.
—JAMES BROWN, TO FELIX HERNANDEZ, HOST OF *THE RHYTHM REVIEW* ON JAZZ 88.3 FM, WBGO, NEWARK

• • •

I didn't have any inhibitions. I saw Elvis and Gene Vincent, and I thought, well, I can do this. And I liked doing it. It's a real buzz, even in front of twenty people, to make a complete fool of yourself. But people seemed to like it. And the thing is, if people started throwing tomatoes at me, I wouldn't have gone on with it. But they all liked it, and it always seemed to be a success, and people were shocked. I could see it in their faces.
—MICK JAGGER

• • •

I say, play your own way. Don't play what the public wants. . . . You play what you want, and let the public pick up on what you are doing, even if it does take them fifteen, twenty years.
—THELONIOUS MONK

• • •

Applause is a receipt, not a note of demand.
—ARTUR SCHNABEL

• • •

I think that when you choose to play music in front of people, you have the responsibility to put on a show. I don't want to spend my money to go see a group of musicians who remain among themselves. . . . I like musicians who look at the public. . . . You have to bring the music to the largest number. Otherwise, well [the jazz players] stay in the clubs. Jazz must be accessible to everyone.

—DEE DEE BRIDGEWATER, JAZZ VOCALIST

• • •

I'll play it first and tell you what it is later.

—MILES DAVIS

• • •

I gained a lot of freedom working with Miles Davis and also a sense of responsibility. . . . Every time we went up there, we had to be in charge of that freedom. [Miles would say,] "Long as everybody can hold up their end." In other bands, that didn't even exist.

—WAYNE SHORTER

• • •

There have been times when I've prayed for a bus to hit me so I'd have an excuse not to perform.

—LINDA RONSTADT

• • •

Remember, they see you before they hear you.
—ART BLAKEY, DRUMMER, ON WHY MUSICIANS SHOULD
LOOK SHARP ON STAGE, AS TOLD BY BOBBY SANABRIA,
PERCUSSIONIST

• • •

I would advise you to keep your overhead down, avoid a major
drug habit, play every day and take it in front of other people.
They need to hear it, and you need them to hear it.
—JAMES TAYLOR

• • •

We love you madly.
—DUKE ELLINGTON, TO THE AUDIENCE

• • •

One more time. . . .
—COUNT BASIE
This can be heard at the end of the song "April in Paris."

• • •

All my concerts had no sounds in them; they were completely
silent. People had to make up their own music in their minds!
—YOKO ONO

• • •

Sobbing idiots.
—MICHELLE TAYLOR, MANAGER TO VIOLINIST REGINA
CARTER
Upon seeing Regina Carter play the Guarneri violin played by Nic-colò Paganini.
Michelle was one of the heaviest sobbers.

• • •

I am not handsome, but when women hear me play, they come crawling to my feet.
—NICCOLÒ PAGANINI

• • •

The roar of the crowd, the intensity that happens when you're in an arena, is overwhelming. It's one of those things you want to have every night.
—EMILY ROBISON, SINGER, THE DIXIE CHICKS, ON THE
COUNTRY TRIO'S PREFERENCE FOR PLAYING INDOOR ARENAS
RATHER THAN OUTDOOR AMPHITHEATERS

• • •

The public is used to hearing it mic'd and with the mechanical reverbatron or all that. . . . It's a shock to hear a voice when it's natural, when it's raw. No glitz. And funny thing, that's the one thing I do that people always remember. Because they have to listen harder. Because it's real.
—TONY BENNETT, ON SINGING WITHOUT A MICROPHONE IN
RADIO CITY MUSIC HALL

• • •

Applause is the fulfillment. . . . Once you get on stage, everything is right. I feel the most beautiful, complete, fulfilled. I think that's why, in the case of noncompromising career women, parts of our personal lives don't work out. One person can't give you the feeling that thousands of people give you.
—Leontyne Price

Price had debuted at the Metropolitan Opera House in 1961, where she received a rapturous forty-two-minute ovation for her performance as Leonora in Il Trovatore.

• • •

We got this encore from half a million people. I had never heard anything like that, or close to that, in my life. Man, every hair on my body was standing on edge. That was when we shifted into a gear that none of us had ever shifted into.
—Sly Stone

• • •

I love performing. I shall perform until the day I die.
—Josephine Baker

• • •

You know, too many flowers in the garden stink.

—Mario Bauzà to Mario Grillo (Machito's son), as told by Bobby Sanabria, percussionist
Grillo was playing bongo on a record date, and Bauzá had stopped him for playing too many licks.

• • •

Ah, Ah, Ah-Ah-Ah-Ahhhh . . .
—Andy Bey, pianist and Vocalist, counting off the beat before performing

• • •

Ray Brown's trio, featuring Milt "Bags" Jackson, had just finished performing a concert in Japan, and Bags had played wonderfully. As Bags walked down the corridor with Benny Green to their dressing room, Benny said to him, "Milt, I just want to know how it feels to swing like that?" Without batting an eye, Bags turned around, looked at him, and said with a smile, "Natural."

• • •

Please sir, one fool at a time.
—Drummer Art Blakey, to a heckler, as told by Bobby Sanabria, percussionist

• • •

This gentleman is a suppository of rhythmic knowledge.

—BOBBY SANABRIA, PERCUSSIONIST
Sanabria committing a faux pas while introducing Candida to the stage to sit in with Bobby's big band at the jazz club Birdland.

• • •

Already too loud!

—BRUNO WALTER, AT HIS FIRST REHEARSAL WITH AN AMERICAN ORCHESTRA, ON SEEING THE PLAYERS REACHING FOR THEIR INSTRUMENTS

• • •

In the 70s, there was a whole new culture below 14th Street [in New York City]. Something was going on every single night. It was always the same three hundred people in the audience, but playing for them, you could experiment and really develop something.

—LAURIE ANDERSON

• • •

I usually take my hands out of my pockets.

—BUDDY RICH, ON HOW HE WARMS UP

• • •

Stay the fuck out of the trumpet section!

—Victor Paz, To a saxophonist
*A saxophonist had commented on how the trumpets should play
a passage in a rehearsal with Mario Bauzá's Afro-Cuban Jazz
Orchestra. As told by Bobby Sanabria, percussionist.*

• • •

I cannot tell you how much I love to play for people. Would you
believe it—sometimes when I sit down to practice and there is
no one else in the room, I have to stifle an impulse to ring for the
elevator man and offer him money to come in and hear me.

—Arthur Rubinstein

• • •

If I don't practice for one day, I know it; if I don't practice for
two days, the critics know it; if I don't practice for three days, the
audience knows it.

—Ignacy Jan Paderewski, cellist

• • •

CHAPTER 7

On Humor

[I think] humor is incredibly important. . . . You have to be able to laugh at yourself and your place in the universe. . . . For me, life would be so empty without humor. . . . It would be like life without music.
—JERRY GARCIA

• • •

It costs a lot of money to look this cheap.
—DOLLY PARTON

• • •

Honey, I've been a hit in so many flops, just once I'd love to be a flop in a hit.
—PEARL BAILEY, SPEAKING OF HER ROLES IN FILMS, AS TOLD BY PAULA WEST, SINGER

• • •

This must be Fats Waller's blood. I'm getting high.
—EDDIE CONDON, WHEN ILL AND GIVEN A BLOOD TRANSFUSION

• • •

A lot of fellows nowadays have a BA, MD, or PhD. Unfortunately, they don't have a J-O-B.
—FATS WALLER

• • •

What comes first, the melody or the lyric? The check!
—RICHARD RODGERS

• • •

I'd rather have a bottle in front 'a me than a frontal lobotomy.
—TOM WAITS, WHEN ASKED ABOUT HIS LIFE'S PREFERENCES, AS TOLD BY GARY WALKER, *WEEKDAY MORNING* HOST ON JAZZ 88.3 FM, WBGO, NEWARK

• • •

There's a great woman behind every idiot.
—JOHN LENNON, ON YOKO ONO

• • •

All the inspiration I ever needed was a phone call from a producer.
—COLE PORTER

• • •

Don't forget after the concert to purchase my latest record. Remember, if you don't like it, you can always give it to someone you don't like.
—SLIDE HAMPTON, TROMBONIST AND BANDLEADER, AT ONE OF HIS PERFORMANCES, AS TOLD BY BOBBY SANABRIA, PERCUSSIONIST

• • •

Harpists spend half their life tuning and the other half playing out of tune.
—ANONYMOUS

• • •

An oboe is an ill wind that nobody blows good.
—BENNETT CERF

• • •

Never look at the trombones, it only encourages them.
—RICHARD STRAUSS

• • •

GENE LEES: How do you tell yourselves apart?
ART FARMER (WITHOUT A TRACE OF A SMILE): When I get up in the morning, if I pick up the bass and if I can't play it, I must be Art.
Lees had asked trumpeter Art Farmer about his twin brother, Addison, who played the bass.

• • •

I guess that he's doing better now. . . . He's dead.
—GERALD WILSON, BAND LEADER AND COMPOSER, AS TOLD BY LUIS BONILLA, TROMBONIST
This comment was made in response to some musicians asking Wilson how Albert Marx, head of Discovery Records, who had been ill, had been feeling.

• • •

I really don't know whether any place contains more pianists than Paris, or whether you can find more asses and virtuosos anywhere.
—FREDERIC CHOPIN

• • •

This gig pays too little for me to be nervous.
—FRANK WESS, SAXOPHONIST, AS TOLD BY BILL CHARLAP

• • •

If it ain't one thing . . . it's two.
—Mulgrew Miller, pianist

• • •

Thank you for the great blow job.
—Anonymous, as told by Harry Allen, saxophonist
This comment was made by a man with a thick German accent, when Allen had finished a set at the Jazzland club in Vienna, Austria.

• • •

I've come to the conclusion that there's no partnership in the ownership of the Mothership.
—The judge at the end of the trial, during the breakup of Parliament-Funkadelic

• • •

People who know jazz guitarist Russell Malone know that he often tells dirty jokes. When he told one of his jokes at a jazz club in the presence of the late pianist, Tommy Flanagan—who was known for his dry humor and quick wit—Flanagan responded with: "Russell Malone . . . Leave it alone."

• • •

On Humor

Junior Cook had some wine and a man asked him to share it with him. Junior's first response was, "No." The guy kept bothering him. Finally Junior said, "Okay, I'll let you take a swig, but, you know, I'm a professional."
—AS TOLD BY DR. LONNIE SMITH, ORGANIST

• • •

DIZZY GILLESPIE: Dizzy no peaky pani.
CHANO POZO: I no peaky engli, but boff peak African.

• • •

Someone had asked bassist James "Jimmy" Woode for a loan. His response: "No, I can't. . . . All my money is tied up in cash."
—AS TOLD BY KENNY BARRON, PIANIST

• • •

It's said God created rock 'n' roll and porno for one reason . . . so ugly guys could get laid, too.
—KID ROCK

• • •

CHAPTER 8

On Spirituality

The aim and final reason of all music should be nothing else but the Glory of God and the refreshment of the spirit.
—Johann Sebastian Bach

• • •

The only good thing to come out of religion was the music.
—George Carlin

• • •

Our music—gospel music—has always been a comfort to those who are looking for some kind of encouragement in their lives.
—Yolanda Adams

• • •

I believe in prayer. It's the best way we have to draw strength from heaven.
—JOSEPHINE BAKER

• • •

Music is an outburst of the soul.
—FREDERICK DELIUS

• • •

Do you know that our soul is composed of harmony?
—LEONARDO DA VINCI

• • •

Hell is full of musical amateurs.
—GEORGE BERNARD SHAW

• • •

I'd rather laugh with the sinners than cry with the saints—sinners have much more fun.
—BILLY JOEL

• • •

If I'm going to hell, I'm going there playing the piano.
—JERRY LEE LEWIS

• • •

The subconscious is often impressed through music. Music has a fourth-dimensional quality and releases the soul from imprisonment. It makes wonderful things seem possible, and easy of accomplishment!

—Florence Scovel Shinn

• • •

If you sit still long enough, a butterfly might come and sit on your shoulder.

—Albert "Tootie" Heath, drummer, quoting his mother

• • •

Rahsaan was the first to open my eyes that performing was a spiritual thing. Every night he'd open himself up to the audience. It was like communion or a religious service. His message was simple: You've got to respect the music and keep telling folks where it comes from. Rahsaan always had a way of making me remember that I didn't get here by myself. Sharing what you know is as important as performing. We're only here for a minute.

—Grover Washington, Jr., on Rahsaan Roland Kirk

• • •

I think that everybody has his or her own experience with God. Even as a kid, when something goes wrong with your life, you're busy blaming God. I believe that when things are going right for rappers, they think that God is blessing them or trying to figure out what they should be doing to get God to bless them.
—REV. RUN OF RUN DMC, TO CHARLIE BRAXTON, MUSIC JOURNALIST AND CULTURAL CRITIC

• • •

The more you know about the whole, the heavier the one thing you eventually get to will be.
—CLIFFORD JORDAN, TO MIKE LEDONNE

• • •

Real music—God-given music—won't fade. Look at Lauryn Hill. I wore her record out. And Johnny Lang—that's a kid who takes pride in what he does. It has to do with vibrations and God. If you get into God, if you love and respect all things equally, what comes out of you musically will emulate that. A kid with a spiritual foundation can figure out the truth.
—PRINCE

• • •

I have my own particular sorrows, loves, delights; and you have yours. But sorrow, gladness, yearning, hope, love, belong to all of us, in all times and in all places. Music is the only means whereby we feel these emotions in their universality.
—H. A. OVERSTREET

• • •

Thank God for those twins called *grace* and *mercy.*
—RICHARD SMALLWOOD

• • •

Music is self-expression. Singing is how I pray, and the music is my religion.
—CHAKA KHAN

• • •

Music gives a soul to the universe.
—PLATO

• • •

Music is God's gift to man, the only art of Heaven given to Earth, the only art of Earth we take to Heaven.
—WALTER SAVAGE LANDOR

• • •

I let nature take its course. I don't sit at the piano and think, *I'm going to write the greatest song of all time.* . . . It has to be given to you. I believe it's already up there before you are born, and then it drops right into your lap. It's the most spiritual thing in the world. . . . Sometimes I feel guilty putting my name on the songs . . . because it's as if the heavens have done it already.
—MICHAEL JACKSON

• • •

I think that all people are soul—not that you are a person that has a soul, but you are a soul that lives in a body.
—RODNEY JONES, JAZZ GUITARIST

• • •

It's not a question of Indian music or American music. Any kind of music, in rhythm, in tune, gives you food for your soul.
—ALI AKBAR KHAN

• • •

I want you to all come to the front of the stage. Ladies, take your pocketbooks with you—everybody around you is not saved, y' know.
—JAMES CLEVELAND, AT A CONCERT, AS TOLD BY ERIC REED, PIANIST

• • •

Facts an' facts, an' t'ings an t'ings: dem's all a lotta fockin' bullshit. Hear me! Dere is no truth but de one truth, an' that is the truth of Jah Rastafari.
—BOB MARLEY

• • •

CHAPTER 9

On the Business

I am amazed at radio DJs today. I am firmly convinced that AM on my radio stands for Absolute Moron. I will not begin to tell you what FM stands for.
—JASPER CARROTT

• • •

Friends don't let friends get into radio.
—DUGG COLLINS, OF KFDI IN WICHITA, KANSAS, AND A MEMBER OF THE COUNTRY MUSIC DISC JOCKEY HALL OF FAME

• • •

If you're in jazz and more than ten people like you, you're labeled commercial.
—HERBIE MANN

• • •

One night it's two police cars stop me and ask me where I got all my money. Say, "Where you been stealing?" I just show them this guitar and tell 'em, "This makes my living."
—LIGHTNIN' HOPKINS

• • •

Always read the small print, because it is never good news.
—RAY BROWN, TO JAMES WILLIAMS, PIANIST

• • •

Either be about it or be without it.
—AWILDA RIVERA, HOST OF *WEEKDAY EVENING JAZZ* AND THE *LATIN JAZZ CRUISE* ON JAZZ 88.3 FM, WBGO, NEWARK, TALKING ABOUT PEOPLE WHO DO NOT TAKE THEIR JOBS SERIOUSLY, THEN LOSE THEM

• • •

I love the record business. It is the thing I do best. . . . There was something that Paul Simon had said to me. He said, "Begin with what you know. You never know where it will take you." So I went into the record business by starting a record company.
—DAVID GEFFEN

• • •

It's not a business, it's a very expensive hobby.
—Warren Vache, the Younger

• • •

Always be smarter than the people who hire you.
—Lena Horne

• • •

[Musicians] talk of nothing but money and jobs. Give me businessmen every time.
They really are interested in music and art.
—Jean Sibelius, explaining why he rarely invited musicians to his home

• • •

I'm one of those artists who feels like she's been taken advantage of, but I'm not bitter about it at all. I was royally robbed, but I don't care. I am richer than I was before.
—Donna Summer

• • •

The bigger the company, the better your chance of getting those royalty checks. The big companies are more accountable than the small ones. Remember, *B*—it's a business. Ain't nothing but a business.
—Louis Jordan, to B. B. King, when he was thinking about changing labels

• • •

[The music business] is like a mirage. While you in it, you got to make it worth your while, and you've got to do something outside of it that's gonna leave you really stable. In this industry they can love you today and can't stand you tomorrow. Once you get into the business you just gotta [invest]. Even if you don't have a whole lotta money, 100 percent of nothing is not better than 10 percent of something. Music has been a nice job for me. It's been a legal way for me to make money and to meet people who are about business.
—KHUJO, OF THE GOODIE MOB, TO CHARLIE BRAXTON, MUSIC JOURNALIST AND CULTURAL CRITIC

• • •

First goal was to own our masters. Without your master tapes you ain't got shit, period.
—SUGE KNIGHT, TO KEVIN POWELL, JOURNALIST AND SPEAKER

• • •

[In the music business,] everybody gets pimped. You have to decide whether you are going to be a streetwalker or a call girl.
—GEORGE HOWARD, TO RUSSELL MALONE, GUITARIST

• • •

Only sick music makes money today.
—FRIEDRICH NIETZSCHE, IN 1888

• • •

The record industry reminds me so much of high school. . . . You got the cool group of kids from this class. Then everyone else is categorized in relation to that cool group. . . . There is a certain safety in running with those hard-rapping, Chanel-logoed herds—at least for the moment.
—LAURYN HILL

• • •

Show business is not the easiest thing to get into, but if that's what you want, you've got to stick with it. A lot of times, I wanted to go home to Mama. There's been thrills and chills, and ups and downs ever since I've been in show business. It never stops.
—SARAH VAUGHAN

• • •

The naïveness of everything, the business end of it . . . you're just told you sound good, we gonna go in the studio, and we gonna make a record. . . . As far as record royalties, you were never explained this. . . . It was way later that I became aware of what monies I had made or could have made if I had known a little bit more about the business end of what I had done back then. . . . In this business, what you don't know can hurt you, because you don't get to reap the benefits of it.
—IRMA THOMAS, TO FELIX HERNANDEZ, HOST OF *THE RHYTHM REVIEW* ON JAZZ 88.3 FM, WBGO, NEWARK

• • •

CHAPTER 10

On Living, Aging, and Dying

The death of Mozart before he had passed his thirty-fifth year is perhaps the greatest loss the musical world has ever suffered.
—EDVARD GRIEG

• • •

Ever since I was a kid, I been dreaming about dying saving somebody. I feel like I'll probably die saving a white kid. . . . I'm serious, I see me dying . . . getting shot up for a white kid. In my death, people will understand what I was talking about. That I just wasn't on some black-people-kill-all-white-people shit.
—TUPAC SHAKUR

• • •

You don't get to choose how you're going to die. Or when. You can only decide how you're going to live. *Now.*
—JOAN BAEZ

• • •

If you run hard enough and live long enough the wrinkles won't catch up with you.
—HARRY BELAFONTE, IN RESPONSE TO ACTOR DANNY GLOVER ASKING HIM WHAT HIS SECRET WAS TO LOOKING SO GOOD

• • •

Miles [Davis] never looked back. He used to say that if you want to stay young, you can't go back.
—WAYNE SHORTER

• • •

The secret to the fountain of youth is to think youthful thoughts.
—JOSEPHINE BAKER

• • •

I think my fans will follow me into our combined old age. Real musicians and real fans stay together for a long, long time.
—BONNIE RAITT

• • •

No matter what you do . . . no one is getting out of here alive.
—James "Jimmy" Woode, bassist, to Kenny Barron,
pianist

• • •

You can't dwell on the loss, because everyone is going to be
lost . . . so you look at the gain of what [a] person gave to life.
What you got from everyone—and what you gave them. That's
the most important thing in my life today.
—Keter Betts, on the passing of his wife

• • •

I'm always asked, "What about being too old to rock 'n' roll?"
Presumably lots of writers get better as they get older. So why
shouldn't I?
—Lou Reed

• • •

Damn, you wouldn't think two guys would near kill each other
over a gal like Lucille.
—Anonymous

*One night at a club where B. B. King was performing, two men
had begun fighting over a woman named Lucille. Their struggle
caused a fire, and in the chaos, King ran out of the club without his
guitar. Before the building burned down, he ran back inside and
got it. That night, King decided to give his guitar the name "Lucille,"
though he had never met the woman with the same name. He said
of his guitar, "I like seeing her as someone worth dying for."*

• • •

CHAPTER 11

On Being Benny Golson

Benny Golson is a talented composer and arranger whose tenor saxophone playing has continued to evolve with time. After attending Howard University from 1947 through 1950, he worked in Philadelphia with Bull Moose Jackson's R&B band, at a time when it included Tadd Dameron, one of his writing influences, on piano. He came to prominence as much for his writing as for his tenor playing while working with Dizzy Gillespie's globe-trotting big band from 1956 to 1958. Golson wrote some memorable standards during the late 1950s; his two-year stay with Art Blakey's Jazz Messengers was significant, and he later co-led the Jazztet with Art Farmer.

Golson eventually drifted away from jazz and concentrated more on working in the studios and with orchestras, even spending some time in Europe in the early 1960s. When he was in Hollywood, he worked on the TV shows *M*A*S*H, Mission Impossible,* and *The Partridge Family,* and on the movie *Lady Sings the Blues.* He continues to record critically acclaimed albums, and he was able to make a reunion recording with the late Art Farmer and Curtis Fuller in a new *Jazztet.*

Talking with Golson on my MNN cable TV show *The Art of Jazz* (2002) was like talking to a sage who has no notion of his own greatness. He is delightful, unassuming, amusing, and full of wisdom. He is a man who acknowledges the past without living in it. I feel blessed to have gotten to know him a little more personally.

• • •

ANDERSON: You are a person who is perhaps known more for your writing than for your beautiful tenor sound. How did you get into writing? Some of your songs that are part of the jazz idiom are "Killer Joe," "Blues March," "Stablemates," "Along Came Betty," "Whisper Not," and "I Remember Clifford."

GOLSON: I did not set out to be a writer. It happened by default. I was trying to learn how to play the saxophone—that was my intention. I was copying from people I heard: Dexter Gordon, Coleman Hawkins, piano players, trumpet players. It didn't matter what the instrument was, I would memorize it. But then I thought, suppose I could write it down on paper? So, I set to writing it down on paper . . . but I was the only one who could play it. . . . Everything was a goose egg, no bar lines, no stems, not anything . . . nobody could play it. . . . I said, I got to do more, I got to get into it a little more. . . . Then I got very good at it. I could write anybody's solo . . . no matter how difficult it was.

• • •

ANDERSON: Once you developed, how did you get with Art Blakey?

GOLSON: I went in that group as a sub. . . . I came down and I played with him at Café Bohemia and I said, "Man, this is great!" At the end of the night [Blakey] said, "We still have a problem, can you come tomorrow?" After the second night he asked, "You think you can finish the week out?" Before the weekend, he asked, "Can you join the band permanently?" I had just come to New York, and you try to get established, write for singers, do TV commercials. . . . I said, "I'd like to, but I'm getting established, you know? I'm afraid to, because I just got here." So the week ended, and he said, "I know you don't want to go out of town, but I have a week in Pittsburgh. If you go to Pittsburgh, one week would not disrupt your plans, would it?" By the end of the second week, [Blakey] said, "You went to Howard didn't you? . . . I have two weeks in D.C. If you come, that won't hurt your plans too much, will it?"

● ● ●

ANDERSON: At the time you were with Blakey, Bobby Timmons was a Jazz Messenger, and you helped him write a song.

GOLSON: Oh, "Moanin'." We'd finish a tune, people would clap. Before we'd go to the next tune, he'd do a little ramblin' on the piano—the way you hear them do—and he'd play this little melody. He'd always laugh when he'd finish it, it was only eight bars, and he'd say, "It sure is funky."

When we got to Columbus, Ohio, I thought about that, and I said, "Yeah, it *is* a funky tune." So I called a rehearsal. . . . When we got there, I said, "Bobby, you know that tune you play, you got the first eight bars, and the second eight bars, and the last eight bars. Now, if you put a bridge to it, you'll have a song," [Timmons did not like the idea, but he begrudgingly did it anyway.] They played it that night on the bandstand and the crowd loved it. Since it had not been named, I asked Bobby, on the bandstand, "What you gonna call it?" Bobby said, "I don't know. When I think about the song I think of 'Moanin.'"

● ● ●

ANDERSON: Did you know immediately that when people started recording your songs that you had to start thinking about owning your own publishing?

GOLSON: Oh, no, that came later. All I knew was the music then. When I came to town here I was green as anybody else. They got me a few times. . . . You learn after you've been slapped a few times, but then you learn. Eventually I got everything back that I owned—it cost me a pretty penny, but I got it back.

● ● ●

ANDERSON: Do you have a certain approach to your music? You, Horace Silver, Cedar Walton, and Randy Weston—some of you guys have had songs that are part of the jazz standards and classics.

GOLSON: Oh, definitely—when I write, I don't particularly write to satisfy you or him; I write to satisfy myself with the hope that he, or you, will like it. And I'm heavily oriented to melody. Melodies tend to be memorable. . . . I like melody. I like Chopin, I like Brahms, the people heavily into melody.

• • •

ANDERSON: So, you are still having a good time?

GOLSON: I'm still having a good time, you know? I figure I've been blessed. . . . And it took me a while to arrive where I am today. . . . I remember all those hard times, and I appreciate being where I am today. It wasn't easy, it took a while.

The future always has an indistinguishable face. We don't know what the future holds, but if we have talent and we get the opportunity, we can give it a face of our own choosing. If we are ambitious and determined enough, as far as we're concerned—not the world. Hopefully the world will like what we're doing—hopefully, but there is no guarantee of any of that.

• • •

ANDERSON: When you write a song, do you feel in your bones that it will be a hit?

GOLSON: Never. How can I say this is going to be a hit? . . . When I was writing "Killer Joe" . . . I had three different melodies to that tune. It was hard trying to decide on one. . . . But that tune, when I wrote it, at the end of the day, I said to my wife, "What do you think about this?" And she said, "It's boring, it will never make it." And it made it—in a big way.

• • •

CHAPTER 12

On Conducting

I never use a score when conducting my orchestra. Does a lion tamer enter a cage with a book on how to tame a lion?
—DIMITRI MITROPOULOS

• • •

No other movement is so consequential.
—DAVID HAZELTINE, PIANIST

• • •

God tells me how the music should sound, but you stand in the way.
—ARTURO TOSCANINI, TO A TRUMPET PLAYER

• • •

You are there and I am here; but where is Beethoven?
—Artur Schnabel

• • •

A good conductor ought to be a good chauffeur; the qualities that make the one also make the other. They are concentration, an incessant control of attention, and presence of mind: the conductor only has to add a little sense of music.
—Sergei Rachmaninoff

• • •

Conductors must give unmistakable and suggestive signals to the orchestra, not choreography to the audience.
—George Szell

• • •

It is a benefit to have the respect of the ensemble.
—Cedar Walton

• • •

Don't perspire while conducting—only the audience should get warm.
—Richard Strauss

• • •

If anyone has conducted a Beethoven performance, and then doesn't have to go to an osteopath, then there's something wrong.
—Simon Rattle

• • •

On Conducting

Well, he tries.
—Victor Paz, lead trumpeter in a disciplinary
hearing for the Broadway show *CATS*, when asked
if the conductor keeps good time, as told by Bobby
Sanabria, percussionist

• • •

The success of our operas rests most of the time in the hands of
the conductor. This person is as necessary as a tenor or a prima
donna.
—Giuseppe Verdi

• • •

He uses music as an accompaniment to his conducting.
—Oscar Levant, on Leonard Bernstein

• • •

CHAPTER 13

On Rejection and Failure

Rejection is the greatest aphrodisiac.
—MADONNA

• • •

Flint must be an extremely wealthy town: I see that each of you
bought two or three seats.
—VICTOR BORGE, PLAYING TO A HALF-FILLED HOUSE IN
FLINT, MICHIGAN

• • •

When I was an utter flop, I kept having the same dream—that all
my teeth were falling out.
—ENGELBERT HUMPERDINCK

• • •

Over the last three years I've been broke, dumped, and pimped.
—TONI BRAXTON

• • •

There are very few rewards for disciplinarians.
—AHMAD JAMAL, PIANIST

• • •

I made something from nothing, a culture for the kids, and now it's a multimillion-dollar business worldwide. . . . None of those dollars came back to me. . . . But I'm still here. Like my man Elton John says, "I'm still standing."
—DJ KOOL HERC, THE ORIGINATOR OF HIP HOP

• • •

When asked if I had ever been in a program before, I replied, "I was on *Saturday Night Live*."
—GIL SCOTT-HERON, IN RESPONSE TO A QUESTION ABOUT HAVING RECEIVED TREATMENT FOR HIS DRUG PROBLEM

• • •

Most of the times, once you're out of the limelight is when you want to be in it.
—TINA TURNER

• • •

CHAPTER 14

On Success, Fame, and Fortune

I'm dreading the day that I wake up and go, "Oh, my God!" and really freak out.
—MUMBA, POP SINGER

• • •

Winning a Grammy sure helped me get laid.
—BONNIE RAITT

• • •

The definition of success is start at the top and work your way down to the bottom.
—JEFF CLAYTON, SAXOPHONIST

• • •

SID VICIOUS: So you're this Freddie Platinum bloke that's supposed to be bringing ballet to the masses.

FREDDIE MERCURY: Ah, Mr. Ferocious, we're trying our best, dear.

This exchange took place when Vicious, of The Sex Pistols, met Mercury, of Queen, at a recording studio.

• • •

I spent, let's see, thirty-five years in America performing. I've already done it in America; they remember me. I've done some good stuff there. So, now, I'm in another part of the world. If you are not successful in your own country, go where your success is.

—TINA TURNER

• • •

I went from making $55 a week in the mailroom to making $2 million in just five years. It was a quick ride. It gave me what people refer to as "fuck you" money. I could genuinely be fearless about the future.

—DAVID GEFFEN

• • •

I wish people would stop taking pictures of me while I'm eating. I can handle the rest.

—DMX, ON BEING A STAR

• • •

With all this attention, you become a child. It's awful to be the center of attention. You can't talk about anything apart from your own experience, your own dopey life. I'd rather do something that can get me out of the center of attention.
—MICK JAGGER

• • •

Because . . . Mick is a great, great artist, he can be sort of blank as a human being—like a lot of good artists are, like the best actors. It's a sort of emptiness, being not quite centered. It's got something to do with narcissism. It's thinking always in a mirror, living in too many worlds.
—CHRISTOPHER GIBBS, ON MICK JAGGER
Gibbs and Jagger are longtime friends.

• • •

Although I have experienced all the troubles and sorrow which precede success, and although I know how important it is for an artist to be spared such troubles, I realize, when I look back on my early life, that it was enjoyable, in spite of all its vexations and bitterness.
—SERGEI RACHMANINOFF

• • •

I went to New York, I had a dream. I wanted to be a big star,
I didn't know anybody. I wanted to dance, I wanted to sing, I
wanted to do all those things, I wanted to make people happy, I
wanted to be famous, I wanted everybody to love me, I wanted to
be a star. I worked really hard and my dream came true.
—MADONNA

• • •

Fame is an illusion.
—JERRY GARCIA

• • •

I do have big tits. Always had 'em—pushed 'em up, whacked 'em
around. Why not make fun of 'em? I've made a fortune with 'em.
—DOLLY PARTON

• • •

You know you've made it when Benny Goodman's fired you at
least once.
—ANONYMOUS

• • •

I would like to be Maria, but there is La Callas, who demands
that I carry myself with her dignity.
—MARIA CALLAS

• • •

I would rather play "Chiquita Banana" and have my swimming pool than play Bach and starve.
—Xavier Cugat

• • •

My mom's like, "Want me to tell my daughter to stop cursing? Would you like a ride in my Mercedes?"
—Lil' Kim

• • •

Being famous was extremely disappointing for me. When I became famous, it was a complete drag, and it is still a complete drag.
—Van Morrison

• • •

I always want to do something better than *Street Songs,* ya know. My concept is hey, yeah, *Street Songs* is fine, "Busting Out" and the Mary Jane Girls and all that is fine, but let's do something else. Let's do something better, something greater. Let's pray for another level, ya know what I mean? And I hate that legend talk because it always makes me sound like I'm dead.
—Rick James, to Charlie Braxton, music journalist and cultural critic

• • •

If you are going to suck something . . . success.
—MONTY ALEXANDER, PIANIST, TO RUSSELL MALONE,
GUITARIST

● ● ●

If at first you don't succeed . . . suc-cess.
—MULGREW MILLER, PIANIST, TO FELLOW PIANIST ERIC
REED

● ● ●

I never balled an opera singer.
—ZOOT SIMS , SAXOPHONIST, AS TOLD BY MICHAEL BOURNE,
HOST OF *WEEKDAY AFTERNOON JAZZ* AND *SINGERS
UNLIMITED* ON JAZZ 88.3 FM, WBGO, NEWARK, AND
WRITER WHO INTERVIEWED SIMS FOR *DOWN BEAT*
MAGAZINE

● ● ●

You want to make some money?
You got to do your hair like mine.
—JAMES BROWN, TO GEORGE BENSON, AS TOLD BY DR.
LONNIE SMITH, ORGANIST
*James Brown has processed his hair for years.
When he gave George this advice, Benson's hair was curly
(natural).*

● ● ●

Do you know what the secret of success is? Be yourself and have some fun.
—TITO PUENTE, TO AWILDA RIVERA, THE HOST OF *EVENING JAZZ* AND *THE LATIN JAZZ CRUISE* ON JAZZ 88.3 FM, WBGO, NEWARK

• • •

95 percent perspiration and 5 percent inspiration.
—RON CARTER, QUOTING A COMMONLY KNOWN PHRASE, COMMENTING ON WHAT IT TAKES TO BE A SUCCESSFUL MUSICIAN

• • •

Bill Cosby was a frequent guest of Johnny Carson on *The Tonight Show*. It would not be unusual for Cosby to walk on with a jazz musician in tow. One night he showed up with Dizzy Gillespie (who always seemed to make Carson a bit uncomfortable). Cosby started rambling on about this tour that Dizzy was on where he was being paid $50,000 per week, whereupon Dizzy rolled his eyes and interrupted, saying, "You mean 50,000 Cruzeiros!"
—AS TOLD BY BOB PORTER, PRODUCER AND HOST OF *PORTRAITS IN BLUE* AND *SATURDAY MORNING FUNCTION* ON JAZZ 88.3 FM, WBGO, NEWARK

• • •

CHAPTER 15

On Other Musicians

Bach is like an astronomer who, with the help of ciphers, finds the most wonderful stars. . . . Beethoven embraced the universe with the power of his spirit. . . . I do not climb so high. A long time ago, I decided that my universe will be the soul and heart of man.
—FREDERIC CHOPIN

• • •

Leonard Bernstein has been disclosing musical secrets that have been known for over four hundred years.
—OSCAR LEVANT

• • •

If it hadn't been for him, there wouldn't have been none of us. I
want to thank Mr. Louis Armstrong for my livelihood.
—Dizzy Gillespie

• • •

I occasionally play works by contemporary composers, and for two
reasons. First, to discourage the composer from writing any more,
and secondly to remind myself how much I appreciate Beethoven.
—Jascha Heifetz

• • •

Handel understands effect better than any of us—when he
chooses, he strikes like a thunderball.
—Wolfgang Amadeus Mozart

• • •

For me, he was a gentleman on stage. His friendship, his love, and
his treatment towards me is something I will always cherish.
—Celia Cruz, on Tito Puente

• • •

Ella had perfect pitch, but she didn't shade lyrics very often. Her dramatic approach was monochromatic, whereas Billie had so much warmth! She could sing the heaviest, darkest thing with so much heart, and lay every word and emphasize the right ones and really dig the text out so that you know what she was singing about. Ella was more like Mariah Carey. You'd just follow the sheen of the line.

—JONI MITCHELL, ON ELLA FITZGERALD AND BILLIE HOLIDAY

• • •

Without Elvis, none of us could have made it.

—BUDDY HOLLY

• • •

I think she allowed women to have their pain. Her thing was so born from her pain. Her amazing talent was because of the pain she had. . . . I think she was misunderstood, and she was so intelligent, emotionally intelligent, and what came out of her was almost beyond what her physical body could even do as a singer.

—NANCY WILSON, ON JANIS JOPLIN

• • •

Freddie always looked like a star and acted like a star, even when he was penniless.

—BRIAN MAY, GUITARIST, ON FREDDIE MERCURY

• • •

The approach to the piano that Bill Evans had, the orchestration implications he was doing, also gave inspiration to how the overall sound of Weather Report would move, and this is all connected with Stravinsky and Bartok—it's many people, opera too. A lot of the classic composers—Chopin, Beethoven, Stravinsky, they had the spirit of what jazz means, you know. [sings] It doesn't have to be syncopation but . . . Beethoven was syncopating in some places! The word *jazz* to me means *creative music.*
—WAYNE SHORTER

• • •

How do you approach Monk's music? Carefully!
—TOMMY FLANAGAN

• • •

He so naturally and gracefully gave so much of himself, and that was a big part of what made him one of the real singers of the saxophone.
—FREDDIE COLE, VOCALIST, ON GROVER WASHINGTON, JR.

• • •

His jazz trio was the epitome of taste, musicianship, and serious swing. . . . His technique was a miracle of economy.
—B. B. KING, ON NAT KING COLE

• • •

There is no question that he's brilliant—the most gifted composer and performer in popular music today. But I think it trivializes Michael to call him eccentric. He's an incredibly rich and complex human being with both the wisdom of an eighty-five-year-old sage and the magical, childlike curiosity and wonder of a Peter Pan. And the intensity of his creative energy is awesome, like a force of nature.
—QUINCY JONES, ON MICHAEL JACKSON

• • •

All musicians should get together on a certain day and get down on their knees to thank you.
—MILES DAVIS, TO DUKE ELLINGTON

• • •

I once served a steak to Janis Joplin at Max's Kansas City. She was quiet and very polite. She didn't eat the steak but left a $5 tip.
—DEBORAH HARRY

• • •

Charlie Parker was fantastic, a genius on that horn, a genius music-wise. He used to sit on the bus or train with Stravinsky scores. And then he'd get on the stage and play something from Stravinsky, but play it his way. Nobody ever knew that.
—SARAH VAUGHAN

• • •

I got the impression from him that he wasn't playing—he was singing. When you're trying to sing from the soul, that's just how it comes out.
—KURT WHALUM, ON GROVER WASHINGTON, JR.

• • •

[He] was my right arm, my left arm, all the eyes in the back of my head, my brainwaves in his head, and his in mine. He was not . . . my alter ego.
—DUKE ELLINGTON, ON BILLY STRAYHORN

• • •

If I had to describe Bob Marley in a few words, I'd say he was a great lyric writer, a musical genius, and a great leader of men.
—ERIC CLAPTON

• • •

Bob [Marley] is very, very important to the people, and especially if you are a Jamaican. He holds the banner in a mighty way . . . he speaks about the world, he is a messenger, his world, his songs are so lovely, to remember his melody, his words are very inspirational. Someone said "after the Psalms of the Bible, the best person for the world is Bob . . . his songs are like Psalms all over again."
—MONTY ALEXANDER, PIANIST

• • •

She got me to move in next door to her . . . which I did. That's when she started on heavy drugs. . . . She used to shoot it in her arm. . . . She didn't know how to hold the tie . . . you know, that makes the vein stick out. She had to have somebody to hold that. She used to call me, and I'd go over and hold the . . . tie. But I'll tell you one thing . . . she never offered it to me. Because if she had, I would have taken it! I loved her for that . . . years later.
—CARMEN MCRAE, SPEAKING OF BILLIE HOLIDAY TO GENE DAVIS, PRODUCER

• • •

Jackie Wilson was the most incredible artist to grace the stage. Jackie Wilson lived to go on the stage. When he went on the stage he became *alive*. This man was fire!
—RUTH BROWN, TO FELIX HERNANDEZ, HOST OF *THE RHYTHM REVIEW* ON JAZZ 88.3 FM, WBGO, NEWARK

• • •

The basis of our music was rhythm and blues. . . . Ruth Brown was the hippest thing. . . . Ruth Brown made that transition from blues, cold-blooded blues. Ah, let's say that I feel Bessie Smith, Dinah Washington, Ruth Brown slicked it up, and she was Miss Rhythm and Blues, she is the woman that they put the name Miss Rhythm and Blues on.
—ETTA JAMES, TO FELIX HERNANDEZ, HOST OF *THE RHYTHM REVIEW* ON JAZZ 88.3 FM, WBGO, NEWARK

• • •

Horace's music is so dramatic, it fills my need as an actress.
—DEE DEE BRIDGEWATER, JAZZ VOCALIST WHO RECORDED
A CD CALLED *LOVE AND PEACE: TRIBUTE TO HORACE
SILVER*

• • •

School's Out!
—ANONYMOUS, AS TOLD BY HARVEY S. WISE
*This was said when Art Blakey died. He was known for having
been a great teacher and band leader.*

• • •

CHAPER 16

On Love, Passion, Relationships, and Sex

Music is love in search of a word.
—SIDNEY LANIER

• • •

If music be the food of love, play on.
—WILLIAM SHAKESPEARE

• • •

Sometimes it's a form of love just to talk to somebody that you have nothing in common with and still be fascinated by their presence.
—DAVID BYRNE

• • •

Ninety-nine percent of the world's lovers are not with their first choice. That's what makes the jukeboxes play.
—WILLIE NELSON, AS TOLD BY MICHAEL BOURNE, HOST, *WEEKDAY AFTERNOON JAZZ* AND SINGERS *UNLIMITED* ON JAZZ 88.3 FM, WBGO, NEWARK

• • •

Janis Joplin taught me about passion.
—AMY RAY, OF THE INDIGO GIRLS

• • •

Women have way more baggage than men do because they let all the wrong men do their packing.
—ERIC REED, PIANIST

• • •

My attitude toward men who mess around is simple: If you find 'em, kill 'em.
—LORETTA LYNN

• • •

I've usually thought of love as a private matter. . . . Yet once you've
found love . . . you somehow want to share that joy.
—BARBRA STREISAND

• • •

If you find a love that you know nothing about, come and tell me,
and I will experience it for you.
—CARMEN MCRAE, AS TOLD BY JEFF CLAYTON,
SAXOPHONIST

• • •

There are more love songs than anything else. If songs could
make you do something, we'd all love one another.
—FRANK ZAPPA

• • •

Girl, you are San Quentin quail.
—DUKE ELLINGTON
*Ellington's response when a fifteen-year-old girl came to his dressing
room and asked to sleep with him. "San Quentin quail" is another
term for jailbait.*

• • •

Why is age more than a number when it comes to love?
—PRINCE

• • •

Nice eyes, Prez.
—Percy Heath, as told by Lester Young
*Bassist Percy Heath said this at his brother Albert "Tootie" Heath's
sixty-seventh birthday party, when Percy noticed a beautiful
woman walk by. Young said that often when he liked something.*

• • •

I am not in love . . . but I'm open to it.
—Joan Armatrading

• • •

If I had as many love affairs as I've been given credit for, I'd be in
a jar in the Harvard Medical School.
—Frank Sinatra

• • •

At some point in everyone's career, you begin to hear the roar of
the crowd. And when the roar of the crowd drowns out the one
voice that matters, you get lost and you just pray to God you're
found again.
—Angie Stone, on her breakup with D'Angelo

• • •

JEFF CLAYTON: Sweets, I got a girlfriend for you.
HARRY "SWEETS" EDISON: How old is she?
CLAYTON: I don't know, about your age. [Edison was in his seventies.]
EDISON: What do I need with a woman my age? Have you ever seen a seventy-year-old woman with her clothes off?
CLAYTON: Nah.
EDISON: I need somebody to give me some *inspiration!*

• • •

You'll have to ask somebody older than me.
—EUBIE BLAKE, WHEN ASKED, AT THE AGE OF NINETY-SEVEN, AT WHAT AGE THE SEX DRIVE GOES

• • •

The trouble with some women is that they get all excited about nothings—and then marry him.
—CHER

• • •

CHAPTER 17

On Life and Lessons Learned

The past is gone and the future might not even be, the only thing
we ever experience is the now, I try to enjoy the minute.
—GEORGE HARRISON

• • •

Life is what happens while you are making other plans.
—JOHN LENNON

• • •

I never hurt nobody but myself, and that's nobody's business
but my own.
—BILLIE HOLIDAY

• • •

Willie Nelson was engaged in a conversation about the subject matter of broken relationships in quite a few country songs. When the country icon was asked if country lyrics ever provided any life lessons for him, he said yes. With respect to his own relationships, he figured next time he would just find a woman who didn't like him much and buy her a house.
—As told by Gary Walker, *Weekday Morning* host on Jazz 88.3 FM, WBGO, Newark.

• • •

I chose and my world was shaken. So what? The choice may have been mistaken; the choosing was not. You have to move on.
—Stephen Sondheim

• • •

The amount of money one needs is terrifying. . . .
—Ludwig van Beethoven

• • •

One never know, do one?
—Fats Waller

• • •

I started late. I was thirty-something when I made my first record . . . 1954 or 1953. I just wasn't ready! Everything I do in my life is when I'm older, older than the average person who did the same thing.
—Carmen McRae, as told to Gene Davis, producer

• • •

Mediocrity is the enemy of excellence.
—BOBBY SANABRIA, PERCUSSIONIST

• • •

Music, drawing, books, invention, and exercise will be so many
resources to you against ennui.
—THOMAS JEFFERSON, TO DAUGHTER MARTHA

• • •

Get out of the bathroom, someone else has to use it!
—ALLAN HARRIS, JAZZ VOCALIST

• • •

Life gets mighty precious when there's less of it to waste.
—BONNIE RAITT

• • •

A lie may well fool someone else, but it tells the truth about you
to you.
—JOHN WESLEY HARDING

• • •

Birds of a feather . . . bunch up.
—JEFF CLAYTON, SAXOPHONIST

• • •

Bob, you realize that the guy had a gun. . . . You need to deal with the interest and leave the principle alone.
—GIL EVANS
Evans said this to Bob Stewart, in response to Stewart's pushing an armed guard in the airport in Spain in 1976, when Spain was under a dictatorship. The guard had pushed his opened tuba case, and Bob did not react favorably to it.

• • •

The chains of habit are too weak to be felt until they are too strong to be broken.
—JEFF CLAYTON, SAXOPHONIST

• • •

If you have patience and knowledge, and if you are aware of all that is happening around you, you will gain something unexpected.
—ALHAJI IBRAHIM ABDULAI, A DRUMMER FROM NORTH GHANA, AS TOLD BY ERIC RUCKER

• • •

People who make a living doing something they don't like wouldn't be happy with a one-day work week.
—DUKE ELLINGTON

• • •

You need to listen to yourself first.
—Joao Gilberto, To Duduka Da Fonseca,
Percussionist

Gilberto gave Da Fonseca this advice in 1977. Da Fonseca had only been living in New York City, where Gilberto had been for some time, for two years. Da Fonseca played the then-famous club Cachaca, where Brazilian musicians would go to hear each other play. Gilberto's advice is comparable to the expression "If you love yourself first, you will be able to love others."

• • •

Let go of that hate in your heart, it will kill you quicker than cancer.
—Benny Carter, saxophonist and composer, to drummer and former host on Jazz 88.3 FM, WBGO, Newark, Kenny Washington, when Washington was in the throes of a nasty divorce

• • •

CHAPTER 18

On Being T. S. Monk, the Son of Thelonious

Thelonious Sphere Monk is recognized as one of the most influential figures in the history of jazz. He was one of the architects of bebop, and his impact as a composer and pianist has had a profound influence on every genre of modern music. He was criticized by observers who failed to listen to his music on its own terms. Monk suffered through a decade of neglect before he was suddenly acclaimed as a genius; though his music had not changed one bit, listeners' perceptions had.

Thelonious Monk grew up in New York, started playing piano when he was around five years old, and had his first job touring as an accompanist to an evangelist. When he was playing in the house band of Minton's Playhouse from 1940 to 1943, he began searching for his own individual style. Two of his most well-known songs, "Epistrophy" and "Round Midnight," were recorded during that time period.

One of my most memorable television interviews was with Monk's son, T. S. Monk, in 2001. He shared his thoughts and memories of his dad with admiration and love. We also talked about his work as a drummer and about the music industry in general. In addition to being a musician, T. S. is also the Chairman of the Board of the Thelonious Monk Institute.

• • •

ANDERSON: What was it like growing up the son of Thelonious Monk? Were you in awe?

MONK: I had a ball. He did not require me to be anything other than his son. . . . He would say, "Hey, man, is everything cool?" I never tire of questions about my father, because I had a good time and I liked him so much. Anybody you like you like to talk about. . . . I always felt like he wanted me, my sister, and my mom . . . to be a part of his fame, so I always felt on the inside, never on the outside.

• • •

ANDERSON: What did you think about the movie *Straight, No Chaser*?

MONK: I was intimately involved, and also have a great deal of ownership, in it. . . . I want everyone to know that we're not all broke, a few of us are getting paid. What concerned me when we went to put *Straight, No Chaser* together is that I had looked at Hollywood's treatment of jazz over the years, and what I had seen [was that] rather than concentrating on the music, they seemed to concentrate on all those things that were around the music—the drugs, the women, the club scene, the seamier side of the music.

I said to myself, the reason why we remember Charlie Parker is not because he shot dope, it's because of what he played. And we don't remember Billie Holiday because she died in the gutter, we remember her because of what she sang. It seems like what she sang and what he played are success stories, continual success stories—and that's what we need to concentrate on when we make this documentary about Monk. It needs to have a ton of Monk's music and a ton of Monk. And everything else, people can speculate, people can wonder about, people can go research. . . . What was most captivating about Thelonious was Thelonious was this guy and his music, and let's show the guy and play the music, and everything will be all right. The result was probably the greatest jazz documentary made thus far. I'm not trying to toot my own horn—it happened that way because Thelonious is that much.

● ● ●

ANDERSON: The line that I loved the most was the reporter asking Monk what kind of music he liked. Monk said, "I like all music." The man continued asking Monk if he liked country-and-western and other genres of music. Monk then replied, "I think that this guy is hard of hearing."

MONK: Those guys, the older guys [of Thelonious Monk's generation]. . . . Whether it was Monk, or whether it was Miles or Coltrane, they all used an economy of words, and as a consequence, when they said something, they said what they meant. When Thelonious said, "I like all kinds of music," there were no other questions to ask, because he answered the question and he was crystal clear. That is the way Thelonious was, and I found that that's the way that group was, and it really reflects the way they approached the music.

The music was hip as reality. Jazz is reality music. It's not made of the fantasy and fluff of what popular music is and what popular culture is made of. It's a reflection of how you feel at a specific time and in a specific place in the time continuum. It's heavy-duty stuff, but at the same time it's light. . . . It ain't serious, because we can't take life very seriously. That's why the animals get along so well—they don't take life seriously. . . . Jazz is a reflection of how you feel at a given time, and that is why the music is a direct reflection of the reality of everyday. . . . If you do it like the giants did it, to give yourself to it completely, then everything becomes one. So, the things that you say and the things that you play become very specific; there is no difference between the two. . . . With Thelonious, it was easy. . . . It was bottom-line stuff—"Hey man, be hip." That is very clear; you don't have to think about that a whole lot. He wouldn't talk in generalities. Jazz is very specific. I think that its specificity, in particular, is one of those things that fools jazz aficionados in the early years to think that it was an intellectual endeavor.

• • •

ANDERSON: You play the drums and you sing. You sang one of my favorite songs, "Just a Little Lovin'."

MONK: Patricia Barber is a complete musician and a wonderful pianist. I would have never had that performance had it not been for her. Look, I'm a drummer who likes to sing. . . . In fact, what I like to do the most is to sing and to [play] drums at the same time. I've always thought that that was a very, very special gift not a lot of drummers have. But some have it: Mac Fleetwood, Maurice White, Jeffery Osbourne [a drummer for LTD] and, of course, Marvin Gaye was a drummer. I don't mean guys who sort of sat down and played—Marvin Gaye played drums on all those sessions for Motown before he was singing. And, of course . . . in our own music—we have Grady Tate, he set the standard.

● ● ●

ANDERSONS: I've never heard Grady sing and play.

MONK: I felt that [singing and playing], that sort of is the gift, and it keeps me out of the competition. You see—not to say Grady made a mistake—but if I get up off the drums, then I'm competing with Billy Eckstine, Kevin Mahogany, Frank Sinatra. . . . As long as I stay behind the drums, I ain't got no competition.

● ● ●

ANDERSON: You've done R&B music. You've rue the gamut.

MONK: You see, contrary to what people would suppose, in the Monk household we listened to Thelonious, we listened to Coltrane, Miles, Bird [Charlie Parker], Dizzy, and Art Tatum and all those cats. But my father—and any jazz musician would understand what I'm saying—part of your job as a jazz musician is to take in information, to build one's vocabulary as a musician. In order to do this, one must listen to much music, far outside the mere limitations of jazz. You have to listen to country-and-western, rock 'n' roll, you have to listen to gospel, ethnic music. My father did it, Miles did it, Coltrane did it. You can hear this in their music. So, you can tell that there were no prerequisites for the kind of music I could listen to. So, in 1955, as I was listening to Little Richard, I listened to Elvis Presley. In 1963, I was listening to The Beatles, and The Rolling Stones. In 1968, I was listening to Jimi Hendrix and Sly and the Family Stone. I was listening to The Temptations—I heard it all. I grew up with it, and I loved it. If you think about the sound of drums on Motown records, as a musician, if you just listen . . . the sound of the drum on Motown records was fabulous.

• • •

121

CHAPTER 19

On Musical Genres

What is scurrilously called ragtime is an invention that is here to stay. That is now conceded by all classes of musicians. . . . All publications masquerading under the name of ragtime are not the genuine article. . . . That real ragtime of the higher class is rather difficult to play is a painful truth which most pianists have discovered. Syncopations are no indication of light or trashy music. . . . Joplin ragtime is destroyed by careless or imperfect rendering, and very often players lost the effect entirely by playing too fast.
—Scott Joplin

• • •

On Musical Genres

It is from the blues that all that may be called American music
derives its most distinctive characteristics.
—JAMES WELDON JOHNSON

• • •

Blues is a good woman feeling bad.
—THOMAS A. DORSEY

• • •

Maybe our forefathers couldn't keep their language together
when they were taken away from Africa, but this—the blues—
was a language we invented to let people know we had something
to say. And we've been saying it pretty strong ever since.
—B. B. KING

• • •

You don't have to be Mack to play the blues, you don't have to be
poor to play the blues, but you have to eat pork.
—JACK MCDUFF, ORGANIST, TO PETER LEITCH, GUITARIST,
WHILE DRIVING TO A BARBECUE JOINT

• • •

Playing "Bop" is like Scrabble with all the vowels missing,
—DUKE ELLINGTON

• • •

I was really tired of R&B sounding the same, I think Sly [Stone] taught me that. I think that James Brown taught me just unadulterated, ugly-ass, stank, doo-doo funk. But really my recipe was just to explore and innovate all of the music and all of the knowledge that I had. I think that it's important for Black music to always, always grow. We are the original exponents of rock 'n' roll, jazz, and blues. And we've always taken it to another level.
—RICK JAMES, TO CHARLIE BRAXTON, MUSIC JOURNALIST AND CULTURAL CRITIC

• • •

This call cannot be completed as dialed. . . . This line has been disconnected at the customer's request. Black people are strange. Sometimes I think the blues reminds them of a time they don't want to remember. What they've got to realize is that I'm twenty years old. I'm not going to be singing about picking cotton. I don't know a damn thing about it. The blues are alive and well as long as I'm alive and well. I love what I do, I love the blues.
—SHEMEKIA COPELAND, DAUGHTER OF THE LATE JOHNNY "CLYDE" COPELAND, ON YOUNG PEOPLE AND THE BLUES

• • •

Jazz came to America three hundred years ago in chains.
—PAUL WHITEMAN

• • •

Jazz will endure, just as long as people hear it through their feet,
instead of their brains.
—JOHN PHILIP SOUSA

• • •

Milton, of all people, gave the most perfect definition of the state
of mind required to play jazz: "with wanton heed and giddy cun-
ning." That's how you play jazz.
—PAUL DESMOND

• • •

Well, rock 'n' roll was kind of rhythm and blues and boogie-
woogie and swing era. It swung. But when white musicians
started to play it, it didn't swing. They just rocked it, so the beat
got very vertical. White rhythmic history is pretty much funerals,
polkas, and waltzes. Most of the grooves, the drums, come out
for death—either marching to war or marching to the grave. So,
when whites took over rock 'n' roll, the joy went out of it. I never
liked white rock 'n' roll, per se.
—JONI MITCHELL

• • •

Classical music is the kind we keep thinking will turn into a tune.
—FRANK MCKINNEY HUBBARD

• • •

I think classical music kinda cools the spirit, ya know. Like
hearing Miles. . . .
—Rick James

• • •

You're talking to someone who really understands rock music.
—Tipper Gore

• • •

Sixties music is still famous, is still popular and always will be,
because people are still trying to get that feeling those people
had. It came out of their heads, hearts, and had feeling and soul.
That's why they called it soul music; it wasn't contrived, it just
came out of our souls, we just did it.
—Carla Thomas, to Felix Hernandez, host of *THE
RHYTHM REVIEW* on Jazz 38.3 FM, WBGO, Newark

• • •

If it wasn't for rap there would be no poetry in America. I think
we went directly from Walt Whitman to Ice-T.
—Frank Zappa, to Jon Winokur

• • •

Rock is really about dick and testosterone.
—Courtney Love

• • •

The opera ain't over 'til the fat lady sings.
—DAN COOK

• • •

Why, an opera is sure of success when the plot is well worked out,
the words written solely for the music and not shoved in here
and there to suit some miserable time (which, God knows, never
enhances the value of any theatrical performance, but rather
detracts from it). . . . The best thing of all is when a good composer, who understands the stage and is talented enough to make
sound suggestions, meets an able poet, that true phoenix.
—WOLFGANG AMADEUS MOZART

• • •

In opera, there is always too much singing.
—CLAUDE DEBUSSY

• • •

Opera in English is, in the main, just about as sensible as baseball
in Italian.
—H. L. MENCKEN

• • •

Country music is three chords and the truth.
—HARLAN HOWARD

• • •

On Musical Genres

I've always felt rock 'n' roll was very, very wholesome music.
—ARETHA FRANKLIN

• • •

The way I see it, rock 'n' roll is folk music.
—ROBERT PLANT

• • •

Lately, I have been learning bluegrass tunes, and it amazes me how good bluegrass players will improvise around the shape of a melody. The melodies stay within one scale, but they are so active. Trying to improvise and keep that intact is one of those mysteries that I don't think I'll solve in this life.
—BILL FRISELL, GUITARIST

• • •

Gut bucket, deep bass, and funky guitar. The others did not have that. We had the bottom to it, what you called funk.
—RUFUS THOMAS, TO FELIX HERNANDEZ, HOST OF *THE RHYTHM REVIEW* ON JAZZ 88.3 FM, WBGO, NEWARK

• • •

Like blues, the samba is an "invention" from black African prisoners interned in the huge South American plantations, the famous latifundias. But if the blues is sad like a cotton field, samba is cheerful, furious, and sunny.
—ANTONIO CARLOS "TOM" JOBIM, COMPOSER, SONGWRITER, AND ARRANGER

• • •

My definition of Latin jazz is jazz music combined with our Latin rhythms. It's a marriage of both musics, the modern conception of jazz's harmonic and melodic aspects, combined with our Latin percussion instruments, our basic cultural instruments. It reflects the strength of the roots of both musics. I think that creates excitement, that combination, and it's unique within the jazz tradition.

—TITO PUENTE, PERCUSSIONIST

• • •

I've always been a Latin [music] freak. I realized that our music and that of our Latin American brothers had a common source. The Latin musician was fortunate in one sense. They didn't take the drum away from him, so he is polyrhythmic.

—DIZZY GILLESPIE

• • •

I think that the quajira and the blues are linked by powerful links. They are the fruit of the workers, of those which cut canes in Cuba and Puerto Rico, or of those which pick cotton in the Deep South. Music, ultimately, is the reflection of these people, and is more beautiful when springing up from the people.

—RAY "HARD HANDS" BARRETTO

• • •

On Musical Genres

Salsa was a name given to Cuban music in the 1960s in New York. At that time, a lot of Cuban orchestras were playing, and they gave it that name as a kind of commercial name. In general, it's called Cuban music, but there were different rhythms, like the rumba, guaguanco, cha-cha-cha, son. Today all those rhythms together are called salsa.

—Celia Cruz, "The Queen of Salsa"

• • •

The word salsa combines all kinds of music into one, like the mambo, the cha-cha, the merengue, all music with Caribbean origins. When they call it salsa, you don't actually define what rhythm is. That's why I don't particularly care for the word. However, sometimes they call me "The King of Salsa," so I'll go along with it, I won't dispute it—as long as they don't call me "The Queen of Salsa"!

—Tito Puente

• • •

Reggae music is simple music—but it's from the heart. Just as people need water to drink, people also need music. If it is true music, the people will be drawn to it.

—Ziggy Marley

• • •

A marriage of R&B and all influences, but the beat was the same—Ska is a tempo that is generally blues-based, and just the way Jamaicans felt the beat, the ska [he demonstrates] is the after beat.
—MONTY ALEXANDER
Growing up in Jamaica, West Indies, Alexander listened to American music, mostly that from New Orleans.

• • •

Rappers are fearless. We have the power to generate thoughts, make people second guess the system. So, of course, I become an enemy of the system when I talk about the system. . . . And maybe that's what really scares people about rap—not that it has the power to stir up trouble, but that it makes us think about troubles we'd just as soon shove under the table.
—ICE CUBE

• • •

Yeah, that's what it comes down to. To me, music is such a beautiful thing that you can't shut off no particular brand of music. If you feel it's funky, just implement it, man. I mean that's what Hip Hop was about anyway; just taking bits and pieces of music and recreating and twisting it and making it your own.
—COMMON, TO CHARLIE BRAXTON, MUSIC JOURNALIST AND CULTURAL CRITIC

• • •

CHAPTER 20

On Cynicism

I hate music, especially when it's played.
—Jimmy Durante

• • •

Parsifal is the kind of opera that starts at six o'clock.
After it has been going three hours, you look at your watch
and it says 6:20.
—David Randolph

• • •

The Detroit String Quartet played Brahms last night. Brahms
lost.
—Bennett Cerf

• • •

Once I put it down, I couldn't pick it back up . . .
—RUSSELL MALONE, GUITARIST, DISCUSSING A CD HE
DIDN'T LIKE

• • •

When she started to play, Steinway himself came down personally and rubbed his name off the piano.
—BOB HOPE, ON COMEDIENNE PHYLLIS DILLER

• • •

I think popular music in this country is one of the few things in
the twentieth century that has made giant strides in reverse.
—BING CROSBY

• • •

It's pretty clear now that what looked like it might have been
some kind of counterculture is, in reality, just the plain old chaos
of undifferentiated weirdness.
—JERRY GARCIA

• • •

I had an incredible loathing of rock 'n' roll. If you liked jazz, you
didn't touch rock 'n' roll.
—CHARLIE WATTS

• • •

I worry that the person who thought up Muzak may be thinking up something else.
—LILY TOMLIN

• • •

I love Wagner, but the music I prefer is that of a cat hung by its tail outside a window and trying to stick to the panes of glass with its claws.
—CHARLES BAUDELAIRE

• • •

Wagner's music is better than it sounds.
—MARK TWAIN

• • •

Opera is when a guy gets stabbed in the back, and instead of bleeding, he sings.
—ED GARDNER

• • •

One can't judge Wagner's opera *Lohengrin* after a first hearing, and I certainly don't intend hearing it a second time.
—GIOACCHINO A. ROSSINI

• • •

Musical people are so absurdly unreasonable. They always want one to be perfectly dumb at the very moment when one is longing to be absolutely deaf.
—OSCAR WILDE

• • •

Saxophonist Lou Donaldson, who is known for being vocal about everything, went to the Village Vanguard jazz club to see a performance of another saxophonist (either David Murray or James Carter). Not liking the music much, he asked the owner, Lorraine Gordon, how much she charged people to get into the club. She told him, "$20." Upon hearing this, Lou, in his high, squeaky, southern voice, told her, "Lorraine, you got it all wrong, you need to let the people in for free and make them pay you to get out!"
I don't want to hear this. Turn it off. Really, I don't wanna hear anymore. And I don't want [the audience] to hear this.
—FREDDIE HUBBARD, TRUMPETER
This was said during a live blindfold test, conducted by Down Beat magazine, of the song "Epistrophy" from a Russell Gunn CD.

• • •

Buddy Rich checked into a hospital. The admitting nurse who filled out his admission form asked if he was allergic to anything. He replied, "country-and-western music."

• • •

That record wasn't released, it *escaped*!
—LOU DONALDSON, SAXOPHONIST, AS TOLD BY ERIC REED, PIANIST, IN RESPONSE TO ONE OF PIANIST JASON MORAN'S RECORDS

• • •

Shut the fuck up! We're trying to make some music down here! Jive-ass motherfuckers.
—JOHN ZORN, TO VACLAV HAVEL, PRESIDENT OF THE CZECH REPUBLIC; U.S SECRETARY OF STATE MADELINE ALBRIGHT; LAURIE ANDERSON; AND LOU REED, WHO WERE TALKING DURING A BAR KOKHBA SHOW AT THE KNITTING FACTORY

• • •

GENE SIMMONS: All of us are bandits. We got away without working for a living. That's what it's about.
KID ROCK: For those of us who do play and sing—we can write, produce, play, go out. We can delegate what we wanna do, which in no other field, really, can you do that.
Gene Simmons, of KISS, and Kid Rock discussing the music business on Politically Incorrect with Bill Maher.

• • •

Too many pieces of music finish too long after the end.
—IGOR STRAVINSKY

• • •

CHAPTER 21

On the Nature of Music

There is geometry in the humming of the strings. There is music in the spacing of the spheres.

—PYTHAGORAS

• • •

John Coltrane felt that music is a universe. And this feeling has influenced me too. It's like you see the stars in the sky and know that behind the ones you can see, there are many more you can't see. . . . Whatever there was to say, Coltrane said it.

—McCOY TYNER

• • •

This human thing in instrumental playing has to do with trying to get as much human warmth and feeling into my work as I can. I want to say more on my horn than I ever could in ordinary speech.
—ERIC DOLPHY

• • •

There is something suspicious about music, gentlemen. I insist that she is, by her nature, equivocal. I shall not be going too far in saying at once that she is politically suspect.
—THOMAS MANN

• • •

Music rearranges your molecular structure.
—CARLOS SANTANA

• • •

Music washes away from the soul the dust of everyday life.
—BERTHOLD AUERBACH

• • •

You know what's the loudest noise in the world, man? The loudest noise in the world is silence.
—THELONIOUS MONK

• • •

I think music in itself is healing. It's an explosive expression of humanity. It's something we are all touched by. No matter what culture we're from, everyone loves music.
—BILLY JOEL

• • •

Is it not strange that sheep's guts should hale souls out of men's bodies?
—WILLIAM SHAKESPEARE

• • •

All good music has healing potential.
—HORACE SILVER

• • •

After silence, that which comes nearest to expressing the inexpressible is music.
—ALDOUS HUXLEY

• • •

A painter paints pictures on canvas. But musicians paint their pictures on silence.
—LEOPOLD STOKOWSKI

• • •

Music is a beautiful opiate, if you don't take it too seriously.
—HENRY MILLER

CHAPTER 22

• • •

On Being Oneself

I'm a piano player, a rehearsal piano player, a jive-time conductor, bandleader, and sometimes I just do nothing but take bows . . . and I have fun. My, my, my. My thing is having fun.
—Duke Ellington

• • •

I never wanted to be anything else but what I was. I never tried to sing jazz or classical songs. I sang rock 'n' roll and R&B and blues the whole time. . . . I wanted to sing some ballads. I always wanted to show people that I could sing.
—Tina Turner

• • •

[I'm] a pit bull in a skirt.
—EVE, RAP ARTIST

• • •

Most of it's permanent [my hair], but I do put some pieces at the front to keep it flowing. Do it *myself*, too. I'm a hairdresser—did you know that? I had a barbershop in Newark, New Jersey, for thirteen years. One thing good about my hair is we're a funky band, so even when it's not done and it gets all funky Rasta, it's okay by somebody.
—GEORGE CLINTON

• • •

I was good at that. . . . I could just pick up a different slang word and make a song out of it. I didn't practice, I just had a gift of it.
—JOE TURNER, TO FELIX HERNANDEZ, HOST OF *THE RHYTHM REVIEW* ON JAZZ 88.3 FM, WBGO, NEWARK

• • •

I am a very happy lady that tries to be a good friend. I enjoy what I do, and have always liked it. That's why I'm so happy, and why I want to pass on to others my smile and my happiness. In fact, when somebody asks me how I want to be remembered, I always respond the same way: "I want to be thought of as someone who's always happy."
—CELIA CRUZ

• • •

When you experience change on one level in your life, it affects all the other areas. So I've changed musically. I've also begun projecting a looser appearance than the suit-and-tie image I had when I played with Art Blakey. But I'm still just as elegant and cool.
—Javon Jackson, saxophonist

• • •

[I] did not want a band whose name could be confused with something on the menu (picadillo is a meat and potato hash). [I] changed the name to the Tito Puente Orchestra.
—Tito Puente, on changing the name of his band from Picadillo

• • •

OPRAH WINFREY: Are you pleased with the way you look?
MICHAEL JACKSON: I'm never pleased with anything. I'm a perfectionist: It's part of who I am.

• • •

People want to listen to a message, word from Jah. This could be passed through me or anybody. I am not a leader. [Just a] Messenger. The words of the songs, not the person, is what attracts people.
—Bob Marley

• • •

Beautiful? It's all a question of luck. I was born with good legs. As for the rest . . . beautiful, no. Amusing, yes.
—Josephine Baker

• • •

Look, man, all I am is a trumpet player. I only can do one thing—
play my horn— and that's what's at the bottom of the whole mess.
I ain't no entertainer, and ain't trying to be one. I am one thing,
a musician. Most of what's said about me is lies in the first place.
Everything I do, I got a reason.
—MILES DAVIS

• • •

I was the originator, I was the emancipator, I was the architect
of rock 'n' roll. And didn't nobody want to give me credit for it.
I didn't ask anybody for it because I just made it up and I didn't
think—it's just like if you're barefoot and you make yourself a
pair of shoes. When I made rock 'n' roll I got tired of the old
people's music of that time. I did it because that's what I wanted
to hear. I was tired of the slow music.
—LITTLE RICHARD

• • •

In life . . . I feel like I fall short in just about everything. In music I
can just about do what I need to do. I feel pretty calm most of the
time, but then if I review my situation at all, it always seems like I'm
up there walking the plank. I'm probably a driven person. I always
feel like somebody's cracking the whip, somebody or something.
—BOB DYLAN

• • •

On Being Oneself

I practice when I'm loaded.
—Zoot Sims, when asked how he could play so well
when he was loaded

• • •

I'm driven, even though I don't drive.
—Debbie Gibson

• • •

I think we performers are monsters. We are a totally different, far-out race of people. I totally and completely admit, with no qualms at all, my egomania, my selfishness, coupled with a really magnificent voice. I was the first black diva that was going to hang on. My being prepared is the reason I didn't go away. That is really the substance of my pioneering. Marian [Anderson] had opened the door. I kept it from closing.
—Leontyne Price

• • •

I don't feel that I opened the door. I've never been a great mover and shaker of the earth. I think that those who came after me deserve a great deal of credit for what they have achieved. I don't feel that I am responsible for any of it, because if they didn't have it in them, they wouldn't be able to get it out.
—Marian Anderson

• • •

I don't talk much, because you can't tell everybody what you're thinking. Sometimes you don't know what you're thinking yourself!
—THELONIOUS MONK

• • •

KEVIN POWELL: You mentioned Marvin Gaye in the lyrics to "Keep Ya Head Up." A lot of people have started comparing you to him, in terms of your personal conflicts.

TUPAC SHAKUR: That's how I feel. I feel close to Marvin Gaye, Vincent van Gogh.

KEVIN POWELL: Why van Gogh?

TUPAC SHAKUR: Because nobody appreciated his work until he was dead. Now it's worth millions. I feel close to him, how tormented he was. Marvin, too. That's how I was out there. I'm in jail now, but I'm free. My mind is free. The only time I have problems is when I sleep.

Tupac Shakur was twenty-three years old when he spoke the above words. He was murdered on September 13, 1996, at the age of twenty-five. His CDs continue to sell millions.

• • •

You're talking to the wrong guy to talk about being a purist, because I don't believe in that. I believe in hybrid everything. Whether it's a menu with food, or with women, or whatever. . . .
—QUINCY JONES

• • •

CHAPTER 23

On Song

The high note is not the only thing.
—Placido Domingo

• • •

I never knew how good our songs were until I heard Ella
Fitzgerald sing them.
—Ira Gershwin

• • •

A lot of people are singing about how screwed up the world is, to
hear about that all the time.
—Mariah Carey

• • •

On Song

It is not the writing of the lyric; it is the rewrite.
—Alan Bergman

• • •

I have discovered I should just sing the songs as written and with sincerity. You have to sing like it's a lullaby—and the audience is the baby that you're holding.
—Allan Harris, jazz vocalist

• • •

I love songs about horses, railroads, land, judgment day, family, hard times, whisky, courtship, marriage, adultery, separation, murder. War, prison, rambling, damnation, home, salvation, death, pride, humor, piety, rebellion, patriotism, larceny, determination, tragedy, wordiness, heartbreak, and love. And Mother. And God.
—Johnny Cash

• • •

Blues means a lot of things to different people. A lot of people, they talk about trouble. Blues is about trouble. Different things happen to you in life, what goes on in your world. How you live, how you think, what you do with your life, and how you make out with things that come up that you don't understand, and how you figure 'em out, and how you make out. You can feel happy, you can feel sad. You put all these things in your mind and make up a song about it.
—Joe Turner, to Felix Hernandez, host of *THE RHYTHM REVIEW* on Jazz 88.3 FM, WBGO, Newark

• • •

Why the fuck didn't they leave it alone?
—BILLY STRAYHORN, UPON HEARING NAT KING COLE'S
RENDITION OF STRAYHORN'S SONG "LUSH LIFE"
This was an unusual reaction for the quiet, soft-spoken Strayhorn.

• • •

MICHAEL BOURNE: Is there a song that is so perfect that you play it exactly as it's written?
FRED HERSCH: I would certainly never improvise on "Lush Life."
BOBBY SHORT: And those who have should be shot!

• • •

Anything that is too stupid to be spoken is sung.
—VOLTAIRE

• • •

"Tramp" was one of the songs that Otis Redding came up with because he liked it. He liked those country-blues type songs. He had that feeling, a folk quality, a folk, bluesy feeling in his voice.
—CARLA THOMAS, TO FELIX HERNANDEZ, HOST OF *THE RHYTHM REVIEW* ON JAZZ 88.3 FM, WBGO, NEWARK

• • •

I like an aria to fit a singer as perfectly as a well-tailored suit of clothes.
—WOLFGANG AMADEUS MOZART

• • •

I don't think I'm singing. I think I'm playing a horn. I try to improvise like Lester Young, like Louis Armstrong, or someone else I admire. What comes out is what I feel. I hate straight singing. I have to change a tune to my own way of doing it. That's all I know.
—BILLIE HOLIDAY

• • •

If you can walk you can dance. If you can talk you can sing.
—ZIMBABWE PROVERB

• • •

I have always felt the same way about music, very deep. Every time I come on stage, I feel like it's the first time that I've sung. I always sing with the same spirit and feeling.
—CELIA CRUZ

• • •

There is delight in singing, though none hear it beside the singer.
—WALTER SAVAGE LANDOR

• • •

A voice such as one hears once in a hundred years.
—ARTURO TOSCANINI, ON MARIAN ANDERSON

• • •

On Song

They call my kind of music folk songs. But them no folk songs. Them old blues.
—Howlin' Wolf

• • •

I can't play guitar and sing at the same time. My brain can't handle it. I can't even play rhythm guitar and sing. It's hard enough for me to stay in tune just singing.
—Frank Zappa

• • •

Our sweetest songs are those that tell of saddest thought.
—Percy Bysshe Shelley

• • •

It took me many years to be able to sing, because I wasn't a natural singer. I could carry a tune, but that was about it. . . . As an artist I had been very rigid and cold. When I sang in Mississippi, in a church there, my heart just broke. When I was with my own people, I began to be a better artist and performer. I turned my prejudice loose.
—Lena Horne

• • •

The first [song] I ever recorded was the blues. I called it pretty music but the old people called it the blues.
—Stevie Wonder, to Felix Hernandez, host of THE RHYTHM REVIEW on Jazz 88.3 FM, WBGO, Newark

• • •

I sought higher aspirations. I wanted more. . . . I sang to the very God-conscious person. I celebrated the love of a man and a woman as a couple. I also sang to the wonders of the bedroom.
—TEDDY PENDERGRASS, TO FELIX HERNANDEZ, HOST OF *THE RHYTHM REVIEW* ON JAZZ 88.3 FM, WBGO, NEWARK

• • •

Ray Brown and Milt "Bags" Jackson were rehearsing at Ronnie Scott's club in London. They were going over an arrangement of Sonny Rollins's tune "Doxy." Brown made up a short chorus, which he and Jackson collectively agreed stood fine on its own as a melody. "We don't need to play Sonny's melody," Brown exclaimed. "F— Sonny Rollins!" And that's how he came to title his tune "F.S.R."

• • •

I like singing. I think rap is great. It's great to get away from the normal melodic music that was there before. But I truly do still enjoy a good song. A melody. Good singing.
—TINA TURNER

• • •

Jeff, the writer wrote the notes for a reason.
—BENNY CARTER, SAXOPHONIST, COMPOSER TO JEFF CLAYTON, SAXOPHONIST
Clayton had asked Carter what he thought of his interpretation of a song that Carter had written for him.

• • •

CHAPTER 24

On The Beatles

The Beatles, unequivocally the most influential rock band of all time, introduced more innovations into popular music than any band of the twentieth century. For six years, from 1964 to 1970, they led the music world through their creativity, never losing their ability to communicate their increasingly sophisticated ideas to a mass audience. Their supremacy as rock icons remains unchallenged to this day.

They launched a British Invasion by being the first English group to achieve worldwide stature. *Beatlemania* was not lost on me. At the age of seven, I recall dancing with my girlfriends in my living room to The Beatles' first hit, "Love Me Do." For me, it was love at first listen. My siblings and I sat in excitement as we watched their appearance on *The Ed Sullivan Show* in February 1964. However, my father was not so eager to embrace The Beatles;

he wailed, "They won't last—they are just doing what black artists have done all of these years." Years passed and the boys from Liverpool were still around, eventually winning over my dad. I still remember my shock when he asked me to play the song (he could never remember the title) "She's Leaving Home" from their *Sgt. Pepper's Lonely Hearts Club Band* album.

The Beatles blended all that was good about early rock 'n' roll, and changed it into something original and more exciting. Theirs was a self-contained rock group that wrote and performed its own material. When in the studio, they were instrumental in pioneering advanced techniques and multilayered arrangements. More than just a passing fancy of fame, they proved themselves to be great songwriters and, as composers, they were second to none. Over the years, their songs have had an integral influence on popular music and are increasingly becoming part of the jazz repertoire. Frank Sinatra recorded songs of the Beatles, as did Sarah Vaughan. In recent years Joshua Breakstone, Mulgrew Miller, Eric Reed, and many more jazz artists are sampling from the Lennon-McCartney songbook—some are even recording entire CDs of Beatles music. For certain, their music is here to stay. Now, read in their own words some of the Fab Four's thoughts on music, as well as what others had to say about them.

● ● ●

The guitar's all right as a hobby, but it won't earn you any money.
—JOHN LENNON'S AUNT MIMI, WHO BOUGHT HIM HIS FIRST
GUITAR BUT DISCOURAGED A CAREER IN MUSIC

● ● ●

John Lennon reportedly had a dream in which a man appeared on a flaming pie saying, "You are the Beatles, with an *a*."

• • •

Who the hell are The Beatles?
—ED SULLIVAN IN 1963, WHEN HIS PLANE WAS DELAYED IN HEATHROW AIRPORT DUE TO THE HORDES OF FANS WELCOMING THE BOYS BACK FROM AN OVERSEAS CONCERT

• • •

[The Beatles] is a happy, cocky, belligerently resourceless brand of harmonic primitivism. . . . In the Liverpudlian repertoire, the indulged amateurishness of the musical material, though closely rivaled by the indifference of the performing style, is actually surpassed only by the ineptitude of the studio production method. "Strawberry Fields" suggests a chance encounter at a mountain wedding between Claudio Monteverdi and a jug band.
—GLENN GOULD

• • •

Only Hitler ever duplicated their power over crowds.
—SID BERNSTEIN, PROMOTER

• • •

Q: What do you think of Beethoven?

RINGO: Great. Especially his poems.

Q: What do you think your music does for these people?

PAUL: Uhh . . .

JOHN: Hmmm, well . . .

RINGO: I don't know. It pleases them, I think. Well, it must, 'cause they're buying it.

Q: Why does it excite them so much?

PAUL: We don't know. Really.

JOHN: If we knew, we'd form another group and be managers.

—THE BEATLES' FIRST AMERICAN PRESS CONFERENCE, AT JOHN F. KENNEDY AIRPORT IN NEW YORK CITY, FEBRUARY 7, 1964

• • •

We don't like their sound, and guitar music is on the way out.

—DECCA RECORDING COMPANY, ON REJECTING THE BEATLES

• • •

If being an egomaniac means I believe in what I do and in my art or music, then in that respect you can call me that. . . . I believe in what I do, and I'll say it.

—JOHN LENNON

• • •

PAUL: But we're not anti-religious. We probably seem anti-religious because of the fact that none of us believe in God.

JOHN: If you say you don't believe in God, everybody assumes you're anti-religious, and you probably think that's what we mean by that. We're not quite sure "what" we are, but I know that we're more agnostic than atheistic.

—FROM A 1964 INTERVIEW

• • •

Everything else can wait, but the search for God cannot.

—GEORGE HARRISON

• • •

Christianity will go, it will shrink and vanish. I will be proved right. You just wait. We are more powerful now than Jesus ever was!

—JOHN LENNON

• • •

PLAYBOY: How do you feel about the press? Has your attitude changed in the last year or so?

RINGO: Yes.

PLAYBOY: In what way?

RINGO: I hate 'em more now than I did before.

I am hopeless on discussing style, and technique. I don't even know where the volume is. I was in a music store and this guy came up to me and asked what kind of guitar strings I used. I just told him long, shiny silver things.

—PAUL MCCARTNEY

• • •

DAVID FROST: And when you write music . . . you write it very much, and marvelously, in the current idiom. Do you feel that later on, when you move into another period . . . say in five years time . . . you'll be writing in the same idiom? Or different? Will you change with the times?

PAUL: [chuckles] I think it's just the arrangements. . . . We're not writing the tunes in any particular idiom. So, in five years' time, we may arrange the tunes differently . . . but we'll probably write the same old rubbish!

• • •

LEONARD GROSS: If Lennon is compulsive about anything today, it's about truth as he sees it. But he protests when he's labeled a cynic.

JOHN: I'm not a cynic. They're getting my character out of some of things I write or say. They can't do that. I hate tags. I'm slightly cynical, but I'm not a cynic. One can be wry one day and cynical the next and ironic the next. I'm a cynic about most things that are taken for granted. I'm cynical about society, politics, newspapers, government. But I'm not cynical about life, love, goodness, death. That's why I really don't want to be labeled a cynic.

—FROM A 1966 INTERVIEW

• • •

He was the sage of The Beatles. He found something worth more than fame.

—ELTON JOHN, ON GEORGE HARRISON

• • •

I'm really quite simple. I don't want to be in the business full-time because I'm a gardener. I plant flowers and watch them grow. I don't go out to clubs and partying, I stay at home and watch the river flow.
—George Harrison

• • •

I understand it when I'm Ringo, The Beatle. But when I'm Richie the person, I should be freer. When we were just becoming famous, it was nice to go around to see people knowing you, which is how all famous show-biz people are supposed to do. But it was a drag.
—Ringo Starr

• • •

Of course I'm ambitious. What's wrong with that? Otherwise you sleep all day.
—Ringo Starr

• • •

CHRIS FARLEY: Remember when you were with The Beatles and you were supposed to be dead, and there were all these clues, like you'd play some song backward and it was supposed to say, you know, "Paul is Dead," and, like everybody thought you were dead? That was a hoax, right?
PAUL: That's right, I wasn't really dead.

• • •

As far as I'm concerned, there won't be a Beatles reunion as long as John Lennon remains dead.
—George Harrison

• • •

CHAPTER 25

On Greatness

I've outdone anyone you can name—Mozart, Beethoven, Bach, Strauss. Irving Berlin, he wrote 1,001 tunes, I wrote 5,500.
—JAMES BROWN

• • •

For it is not my business to "earn money," but it is the business of my admirers to give me as much money as I want, to do my work in a cheerful mood.
—RICHARD WAGNER

• • •

This boy will consign us all to oblivion!
—JOHANN ADOLPH HASSE, COMPOSER AND CONTEMPORARY
OF MOZART, AFTER HEARING MOZART'S OPERA *ASCANIO
IN ALBA* PERFORMED IN MILAN IN 1771

● ● ●

Any time truth is recognized, whether it's in art, music, media, it
changes consciousness. When people hear freedom in the music
that we record, that's change. But few people had the creative
control that I've had right from the beginning, to produce myself
and to put out double, triple, even five-record sets.
—PRINCE

● ● ●

I can hear so much real warmth and generosity radiating from
every note that Grover ever played. Besides being such a consum-
mate artist and a unique stylist, it's obvious he was simply quite a
human being.
—HANK JONES, PIANIST, ON GROVER WASHINGTON, JR.

● ● ●

I've been popular and unpopular, successful and unsuccessful,
loved and loathed, and I know how meaningless it all is—there-
fore I feel free to take risks.
—MADONNA

● ● ●

In Portuguese, a *bossa* means a "boss," a protuberance, a hump, a bump. Like you have the bossa of Notre Dame. And the human brain has these protuberances, these bumps in the head. These convexities correspond to the concavities or gray matter in the brain. So, if a guy has a bossa for guitar, that would mean that he has a genius for guitar.
—ANTONIO CARLOS "TOM" JOBIM, COMPOSER, SONGWRITER, AND ARRANGER

• • •

I'd rather be "etern" than modern.
—ANTONIO CARLOS "TOM" JOBIM, COMPOSER, SONGWRITER, AND ARRANGER, TO DUDUKA DA FONSECA, PERCUSSIONIST

• • •

Beyond the sky we fly, perchance to see some greatness there: eternal wonder! That which is born of courage here.
—WAYNE SHORTER

• • •

I never wanted to be famous, I only wanted to be great!
—RAY CHARLES

• • •

Don't bother to look, I've composed all this already.

—GUSTAV MAHLER, TO BRUNO WALTER, WHO HAD STOPPED
TO ADMIRE MOUNTAIN SCENERY IN RURAL AUSTRIA

● ● ●

My voice had a long, nonstop career. It deserves to be put to bed
with quiet and dignity, not yanked out every once in a while to
see if it can still do what it used to do. It can't.

—BEVERLY SILLS

● ● ●

CHAPTER 26

On Society

A true tradition is not the witnessing of a past closed and finished; it is a living force that animates and informs the present.
—IGOR STRAVINSKY

• • •

I am Charles Mingus, half black man, not even white enough to pass for nothing but black. I am Charles Mingus, a famed jazzman, but not famed enough to make a living in this society.
—CHARLES MINGUS

• • •

The great challenge which faces us is to assure that, in our society of bigness, we do not strangle the voice of creativity, that the rules of the game do not come to overshadow its purpose, that the grand orchestration of society leaves ample room for the man who marches to the music of another drummer.
—HUBERT HUMPHREY

• • •

When I was seventeen, an eighty-year-old man named Mr. Lewis gave me some advice regarding education. He said, "Son, always stay hungry for knowledge. Try to educate yourself as much as you can. Learn how to use your mind. If you don't use your mind, the white man will use your back."
—RUSSELL MALONE, GUITARIST

• • •

The mixing of races and the mixing of cultures creates the greatest of all things. . . . Just check out the countries from which the greatest intellectual and artistic giants come. They have always been from countries where a great amount of mixing was going on.
—JOE ZAWINUL, PIANIST AND COMPOSER

• • •

You don't overthrow countries with guns anymore. You buy their banking system. When you buy the economics of the country, you've bought the country.
—KRS-ONE

• • •

For an artist, the whole world is your enemy and lover.
—John Klemmer

• • •

Music and dancing (the more the pity) have become so closely associated with ideas of riot and debauchery among the less cultivated classes, that a taste for them, for their own sakes, can hardly be said to exist, and before they can be recommended as innocent or safe amusements, a very great change of ideas must take place.
—Sir John Hershel

• • •

Hip Hop Nation is no different than any other segment of this society in its desire to live the American dream. Hip Hop, for better or for worse, has been this generation's most prominent means for making good on the long-lost promises of the civil rights movement.
—Suge Knight, to Kevin Powell, journalist and speaker

• • •

Art is the signature of civilization.
—Beverly Sills

• • •

H. L. Mencken once said, "Nobody ever went broke underestimating the taste of the American public." It's probably true. I have a better one. "No matter how carefully and assiduously and how deeply you bury shit, the American public will find it and buy it in large quantity." It's true, absolutely true.
—ARTIE SHAW, AS TOLD BY BOBBY SANABRIA,
PERCUSSIONIST

• • •

We're all trapped by society. Society tells women, "You're supposed to be loyal to one man for the rest of your life." Society tells men likewise, and so on and so forth. It's very exciting, very enticing, for a woman to see a man who simply lives life by his own rules—"I will determine my fate." And so it's very sexy, because somebody feels like an alpha male or an alpha female. They decide for themselves what life is gonna be about.
—GENE SIMMONS, OF KISS

• • •

I wouldn't have turned out the way I am if I didn't have all those old-fashioned values to rebel against.
—MADONNA

• • •

Music and rhythm find their way into the secret places of the soul. Musical innovation is full of danger to the state, for when modes of music change, the laws of the state always change with them.
—Plato

• • •

[The Eiffel Tower] looked very different from the Statue of Liberty, but what did that matter? What was the good of having the statue without the liberty?
—Josephine Baker, on her choice to move from the United States to Paris

• • •

There was never any lack of concern in the black community; there was a lack of direction.
—Gil Scott-Heron

• • •

The rhythm of jazz is against the normal psychological needs of man.
—The Peoples Music Press, Peking, China

• • •

I am against art for mass consumption. Sure, I love consumption!
But the moment the standardization of everything takes away the
joy of living, then I am against industrialization, I am in favor of
all mechanisms that make human life easy, but never the machine
to dominate the human species.
—ANTONIO CARLOS "TOM" JOBIM, COMPOSER, SONGWRITER,
AND ARRANGER

• • •

I hope for a world one day with no more borders, no more flags,
no more wallets.
—CARLOS SANTANA

• • •

CHAPTER 27

❧

On Critics and Criticism

Composers often tell you that they don't read criticisms of their
work. . . . I am an exception. I admit to a curiosity about the
slightest clue as to the meaning of a piece of mine—a meaning,
that is, other than the one I know I have put there.
—AARON COPLAND

• • •

Someday I hope to meet you. When that happens you'll need a new nose, a lot of beefsteak for black eyes, and perhaps a supporter below! Pegler [Westbrook Pegler, a gossip columnist], a guttersnipe, is a gentleman alongside you. I hope you'll accept that statement as a worse insult than a reflection on your ancestry.
—HARRY S. TRUMAN, TO MUSIC CRITIC PAUL HUME
Truman was speaking of an unfavorable review of a performance his daughter Mary Margaret, an opera singer, had been given. Truman hated her music critics and often lashed out at them verbally and in writing. She finally gave up her quest for an opera career to marry.

• • •

I had two separate reviews from the same concert . . . top reviewers. One said I looked great, but I didn't fulfill my capacity; in other words, I didn't sing that good. The other one said I didn't look too hot, but, boy, could I sing.
—SHEILA JORDAN, JAZZ VOCALIST

• • •

Half the critics are frustrated musicians. Or a lot of them want to be out there making the records and aren't. I had one of my reviews on my [latest] record [written] by someone who had no clue about my genre of music. It's like having a classically trained musician go out and critique a rap record. You don't understand it. . . . I remember running into somebody later, and they said, "Oh, don't worry about it, this guy's new. You know, he's just on a learning curve. . . ." Why's he gotta learn on my record for?

—Jo Dee Messina

• • •

Man, we are getting it from all sides. . . . There are some hypo-critical critics who disgust me, men who say one thing in album liner notes and another in reviews. Let me say that I don't think Ira Gitler is one of the hypocritical ones.

—Nat Adderley

As told by critic and author Ira Gitler, in response to his review of the Adderley Brothers' recording The Cannonball Adderley Quintet in San Francisco *as "overfunk." At the time Gitler wrote the critique, the album had sold 25,000 to 30,000 copies (unbeknownst to Gitler).*

• • •

To designate someone a jazz critic and give them a power with the media without the necessary credentials is sheer insanity. They can do serious damage to someone's career. How can you do a technical criticism of an appendectomy if you're not a doctor?

—Ahmad Jamal

• • •

[Monk] has written a few attractive tunes, but his lack of technique and continuity prevented him from accomplishing much as a pianist.
—LEONARD FEATHER
This assessment of Thelonious Monk can be found in Feather's book
Inside Bebop.

• • •

Critics can't even make music by rubbing their back legs together.
—MEL BROOKS

• • •

A musicologist is a man who can read music but can't hear it.
—SIR THOMAS BEECHAM

• • •

Definition of rock journalism: People who can't write, doing interviews with people who can't think, in order to prepare articles for people who can't read.
—FRANK ZAPPA, AS TOLD BY TODD ELDER

• • •

It would be nice if everybody could listen to my music and watch my movies and read my books without anyone telling them how they should think, feel, or accept it, or not accept it.
—MADONNA

• • •

Learning music by reading about it is like making love by mail.
—ISAAC STERN

• • •

I like Wagner's music better than any other music. It is so loud
that one can talk the whole time without other people hearing
what one says. That is a great advantage.
—OSCAR WILDE

• • •

Everybody is talking about Paganini and his violin. The man
seems to be a miracle. The newspapers say that long streamy
flakes of music fall from his string, interspersed with luminous
points of sound which ascend the air and appear like stars. This
eloquence is quite beyond me.
—THOMAS MACAULAY

• • •

Milt "Baggs" Jackson was no fan of fusion music. In fact, he
called it "con-fusion music." On a trip to Europe, he played opposite Weather Report. Upon his return home, someone asked him
what he thought of Weather Report. His response: "cloudy."

—AS TOLD TO MIKE LEDONNE

• • •

If I had something to say, I'd 'a said it.
—Johnny Garry
As told to the author, when I asked him for feedback on my emcee
job at Jazzmobile at Grant's Tomb. He was my first emcee teacher.

● ● ●

Critics make me so angry. I've always said, if you wanna have a really
crappy, lousy record collection, read the reviews. Because critics are
people, especially in music. You know, they're not good enough to be
a musician. And they're too ugly to be a groupie. So they write about
records that are important, as if any record is important.
They don't care about what people really like.
—Bill Maher

● ● ●

CHAPTER 28

On Ignorance

LEW FIELDS: Ladies don't write lyrics.
DOROTHY FIELDS: I'm no lady, I'm your daughter.

• • •

Mine was the kind of piece in which nobody knew what was
going on, including the composer, the conductor, and the critics.
Consequently I got pretty good reviews.
—OSCAR LEVANT

• • •

I don't know anything about music. In my line, you don't have to.
—ELVIS PRESLEY

• • •

I know nothing at all about music.
—RICHARD WAGNER

• • •

I know only two tunes. One of them is "Yankee Doodle," and the
other isn't.
—ULYSSES S. GRANT

• • •

I just played into it, I had a kind of jazz vibrato, but I just played.
Later it struck me that i would like to know what the hell I'm
doing.
—BENNY GOODMAN, REFERRING TO HIS 1938 RECORDING OF
MOZART'S CLARINET QUINTET
*Goodman then went on to study the classical repertoire and in
1940 recorded Mozart's Clarinet Concerto.*

• • •

I remember one day being in a music history class and a white
woman was the teacher. She was . . . saying that the reason black
people played the blues was because they were poor and had
to pick cotton. In response to that comment, I said, "I'm from
East St. Louis, and my father is rich, he's a dentist, and I play the
blues. My father never picked no cotton, and I didn't wake up
this morning sad and start playing the blues. There's more to it
than that."
—MILES DAVIS, TO QUINCY TROUPE

• • •

I'm no expert and have no desire to make myself out to be one. I wouldn't know my mixolydians and dorians from my sweat socks. Nor would I care about distinguishing between a "pentatonic 5th flatted at God-knows-runs and thingamafrazzin' rhythms" and an elephant. What I do know is that this CD moves me. For a musical ignoramus like me, that's enough.
—ANONYMOUS REVIEWER ON AMAZON.COM, ON THE MAHAVISHNU ORCHESTRA'S *BIRDS OF FIRE*

• • •

What I don't understand is how come Elton John does all those foul songs and never gets banned? Didn't he have that one called "Don't Let Your Son Go Down on Me"?
—JOHN WESLEY HARDING

• • •

Americans want grungy people, stabbing themselves in the head on stage. They get a bright bunch like us, with deodorant on, they don't get it.
—LIAM GALLAGHER, OF OASIS

• • •

INTERVIEWER: What shocks you?
MADONNA: Ignorance shocks me.

• • •

CHAPTER 29

On Perspectives and Opinions

The history of modern popular music can be seen, to some degree, anyway, as a series of happy accidents—from Elvis stumbling into Sun Studio to make a vanity record in 1953, to Paul and John meeting at a church festival, to a certain scrawny band from Dublin changing its name from the Hype to U2.

—Dwight Garner

• • •

As long as the white man can label something, he'll keep shit down. If we have an old Ferrari, they say it's beat up, it needs to be fixed. If they have it, it's an antique.

—Miles Davis

• • •

If I want your opinion, I'll give it to you.
—ERIC REED, PIANIST

• • •

The whole disco phenomenon was so big you forget about the
passion of some individuals. The disco format allowed primarily
R&B/jazz-fusion musicians like us to make sophisticated popular
music as long as we had good grooves and beats. It allowed us to
stretch the harmonic possibilities of pop music.
—NILE ROGERS

• • •

I have often thought that if there had been a good rap group
around in those days, I might have chosen a career in music,
instead of politics.
—RICHARD MILHOUS NIXON

• • •

If a man tells me he likes Mozart, I know in advance that he is a
bad musician.
—FREDERICK DELIUS

• • •

In music [the blacks] are more generally gifted than the whites with accurate ears for tune and time, and they have been found capable of imagining a small catch. Whether they will be equal to the composition of a more extensive run of melody, or of complicated harmony, is yet to be proved.
—THOMAS JEFFERSON

• • •

I am positive about life and promote the ideas of happiness and honesty. I know that a lot of people look up to me and copy me, so I'd certainly hate to be doing anything that might be harmful to anyone.
—MADONNA

• • •

New music? Hell, there's been no new music since Stravinsky.
—DUKE ELLINGTON

• • •

While making the recording *Money Jungle* with Max Roach and Charles Mingus, Duke Ellington was sitting at the piano, running over some things. Mingus came over to him and said that they should just play free. Duke looked at him and said, "No, I don't want to go back that far."
—As TOLD BY MIKE LEDONNE

• • •

On Perspectives and Opinions

Among the interrelated matters of a time and place, Muzak is a thing that fits in.
—Chairman of the Board of Scientific Advisors on Muzak

• • •

I mean, you really have to weed through rock 'n' roll to really find something sincere, meaningful, valuable, artistic.
—Wayne Shorter

• • •

The man that hath no music in himself, nor is not moved with concord of sweet sounds, is fit for treasons, stratagems and soils . . . let no such man be trusted.
—William Shakespeare

• • •

You don't need any brains to listen to music.
—Luciano Pavarotti

• • •

phil woods: Why do you look so worried?
duduka da fonseca: Because I didn't like the way I played.
phil woods: Don't worry—after all, it's just music.
Da Fonseca had recorded, with Phil Woods, the album Astor & Elis *for Chesky records.*

• • •

Music should either be done in a church or someone's home.
—Gustav Theodore Holst

• • •

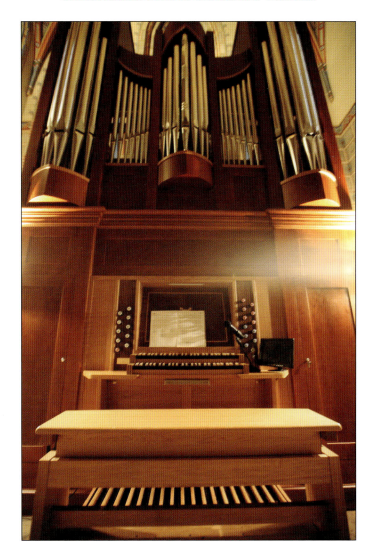

On Perspectives and Opinions

So my dream of becoming a ballad singer is the Apollo inside me.
And I can blame my crazy sex shows on Dionysus.
—MARVIN GAYE, DURING A DISCUSSION WITH DAVID RITZ
ABOUT NIETZSCHE'S *THE BIRTH OF TRAGEDY*

• • •

There are more bad musicians than there is bad music.
—ISAAC STERN

• • •

The people who have the most access to me—people who I've
played music with for twenty years—the fact that they're still
around, either they have the IQ of a plant or I don't have a [drug]
problem.
—GIL SCOTT-HERON

• • •

Nice guys are a dime a dozen! Give me a prick that can play!
—TOMMY DORSEY, IN RESPONSE TO A TRUMPET PLAYER'S
ENDORSEMENT

• • •

What the world really needs is more love and less paperwork.
—PEARL BAILEY

• • •

Dying was a good career move.
—DENNIS OWENS, WGMS RADIO HOST, ON RICHARD
WAGNER

• • •

In my end is my beginning.
—CLARENCE PAUL, DESCRIBING HIS EARLY DAYS WITH
MARVIN GAYE

• • •

I don't like my music, but what is my opinion against that of millions of others.
—FREDERICK LOEWE

• • •

The higher the possum climbs up a tree, the smaller his asshole seems to be.
—HARRY "SWEETS" EDISON, TO JEFF CLAYTON,
SAXOPHONIST

• • •

The end of an error. . . .
—JAMES BROWNE, PROMOTER, OWNER OF THE CLUB SWEET
RHYTHM, AND FORMER HOST OF *EVENING JAZZ* ON JAZZ
88.3 FM, WBGO, NEWARK
*Browne made this comment when general manager Anna Kosof
was fired from WBGO.*

CHAPTER 30

• • •

On Music as Art

I've always told the musicians in my band to play what they *know* and then play above *that*. Because then anything can happen, and that's where great art and music happens.
—Miles Davis

• • •

Music is the art of thinking with sounds.
—Jules Combarieu

• • •

Music expresses that which cannot be said and on which it is impossible to be silent.
—Victor Hugo

• • •

There is no truer truth obtainable by man than comes of music.
—ROBERT BROWNING

• • •

You can play a shoestring if you're sincere.
—JOHN COLTRANE

• • •

It's not about how much you know, it's how much you hear that counts.
—BENNY CARTER, SAXOPHONIST AND COMPOSER, TO IRA NEPUS, TROMBONIST

• • •

You've got to love to be able to play.
—LOUIS ARMSTRONG

• • •

I've always had a divine connection with music. I could feel the good and the evil vibration in music. I was always aware of the power it possessed and the influence it had.
—CEE-LO GREEN TO CHARLIE BRAXTON, MUSIC JOURNALIST AND CULTURAL CRITIC

• • •

So many young cats are trying to play great but nobody is playing good.
—EDDIE LOCKE, DRUMMER, AS TOLD BY PIANIST BILL CHARLAP

• • •

The melody is generally what the piece is all about. The whole problem can be stated quite simply by asking, "Is there a meaning to music?" My answer would be, "Yes." And "Can you state in so many words what the meaning is?" My answer to that would be, "No."

—Aaron Copland

• • •

My own duty as a teacher . . . is not so much to interpret Beethoven, Wagner, or other masters of the past, but to give what encouragement I can to the young musicians of America. I . . . hope that just as this nation has already surpassed so many others in marvelous inventions and feats of engineering and commerce, and has made an honorable place for itself in literature in one short century, so it must assert itself on the . . . art of music. . . .To bring about this result, we must trust the very youthful enthusiasm and patriotism of this country.

—Antonin Dvorak

• • •

The sign of a mature musician is knowing what not to play.

—Dizzy Gillespie

• • •

The notes I handle no better than many pianists. But the pauses between the notes—ah—that is where the art resides.

—Artur Schnabel

• • •

Max [Roach], hands down, is one of the greatest soloists of all time. . . . Max plays musical lines with dynamics and space. What he doesn't play is just as important as what he does play.
—KENNY WASHINGTON, JAZZ DRUMMER AND FORMER HOST ON JAZZ 88.3 FM, WBGO, NEWARK

• • •

If you really want to be an artist, go out and find electricity. It's somewhere.
—BOB DYLAN

• • •

An artist should be judged by his best, just as an athlete is. Pick out my best work and say, "That's what he did, all the rest was rehearsal."
—ARTIE SHAW

• • •

Freedom in music, to me, is the freedom of choice, not playing everything that you know. . . . It is the freedom to play one note— if the note is the thing that moves the heart and touches the soul, that's the note to play. If it is a hundred notes, play a hundred notes.
—RODNEY JONES, JAZZ GUITARIST

• • •

The artist must say it without saying it.
—DUKE ELLINGTON

• • •

Improvisation is too good to leave to chance.
—Paul Simon's father, Louis Simon

• • •

There is so much to be done on earth, do it soon! I cannot carry
on the everyday life I am living; art demands this sacrifice, too.
Rest, diversion, amusement—only so that I can function more
powerfully in my art.
—Ludwig van Beethoven, from his journal, in 1814

• • •

Clouds float in the same pattern only once.
—Wayne Shorter, to Jeff Clayton, saxophonist, on his
own approach to music

• • •

If you want to make beautiful music, you must play the black and
white notes together.
—Richard Milhous Nixon

• • •

Says Who?

Adderley, Nat
Alexander, Monty
Anderson, Laurie
Anderson, Marian
Armatrading, Joan
Armstrong, Louis
Bach, Johann
    Sebastian
Baez, Joan
Bailey, Pearl
Baker, Josephine
Barretto, Ray "Hard
    Hands"
Barron, Kenny
Bauzá, Mario
Beethoven, Ludwig
    van

Belafonte, Harry
Bennett, Tony
Bergman, Alan
Betts, Keter
Bey, Andy
Blake, Eubie
Blakey, Art
Borge, Victor
Bourne, Michael
Braxton, Toni
Bridgewater, Dee Dee
Brown, James
Brown, Ray
Browne, James
Byrne, David
Callas, Maria
Carey, Mariah

Carpenter, Mary
    Chapin
Carter, Benny
Carter, Ron
Casals, Pablo
Cash, Johnny
Charlap, Bill
Charles, Ray
Cher
Chopin, Frederic
Christofore
Clapton, Eric
Clayton, Jeff
Cleveland, James
Clinton, George
Cole, Freddie
Coleman, Ornette

Collins, Dugg
Coltrane, John
Combarieu, Jules
Common
Condon, Eddie
Copeland, Shemekia
Copland, Aaron
Cotton, Elizabeth
Count Basie
Crosby, Bing
Crouch, Stanley
Cruz, Celia
Cugat, Xavier
Da Fonseca, Duduka
Damrosch, Walter
Davis, Miles
Debussy, Claude
Delius, Frederick
Desmond, Paul
Dietz, Howard
DMX
Dolphy, Eric
Domingo, Placido
Domino, Fats
Donaldson, Lou
Dorsey, Tommy
Dorsey, Thomas A.
Durante, Jimmy
Dvorak, Antonin
Dylan, Bob
Edison, Harry
  "Sweets"
Elgar, Sir Edward

Ellington, Duke
Evans, Gil
Eve
Farmer, Art
Feather, Leonard
Fields, Dorothy
Flanagan, Tommy
Franklin, Aretha
Frisell, Bill
Gallagher, Liam
Garcia, Jerry
Garry, Johnny
Gaye, Marvin
Geffen, David
Gershwin, George
Gershwin, Ira
Gibbs, Christopher
Gibson, Debbie
Gil, Gilberto
Gilberto, Joao
Gillespie, Dizzy
Golson, Benny
Goodman, Benny
Gould, Glenn
Grappelli, Stephane
Green, Benny
Green, Cee-Lo
Grieg, Edvard
Hammerstein, Oscar
Hampton, Slide
Harding, John Wesley
Harris, Allan
Harrison, George

Harry, Deborah
Hasse, Johann Adolph
Hawkins, Coleman
Hazeltine, David
Heath, Albert "Tootle"
Heath, Percy
Heifetz, Jascha
Herc, Kool
Hersch, Fred
Hicks, John
Hill, Lauryn
Holiday, Billie
Holly, Buddy
Holst, Gustav
  Theodore
Honegger, Arthur
Hopkins, Lightnin'
Horne, Lena
Houston, .Whitney
Howard, George
Howard, Harlan
Howlin' Wolf
Hubbard, Frank
  McKinney
Hubbard, Freddie
Humperdinck,
  Engelbert
Ice Cube
Jackson, Javon
Jackson, Michael
Jagger, Mick
Jamal, Ahmad
James, Etta

Richardson, Kevin
Richter, Jean Paul
Rivera, Awilda
Robison, Emily
Rodgers, Richard
Rogers, Nile
Ronstadt, Linda
Rorem, Ned
Rossini, Gioacchino A.
Rubinstein, Arthur
Rucker, Eric
Sanabria, Bobby
Santana, Carlos
Schnabel, Artur
Schubert, Franz
Scott, Jill
Scott-Heron, Gil
Seume, Johann G.
Shakur, Tupac
Shaw, Artie
Shaw, George Bernard
Shelley, Percy Bysshe
Shinn, Florence Scovel
Short, Bobby
Shorter, Wayne
Sibelius, Jean
Sid Vicious
Sills, Beverly
Silver, Horace
Simmons, Gene
Simon, Louis
Sims, Zoot
Sinatra, Frank

Smallwood, Richard
Smith, Dr. Lonnie
Sondheim, Stephen
Sousa, John Philip
Starr, Ringo
Stern, Isaacx
Stokowski, Leopold
Stone, Angie
Stone, Sly
Strauss, Richard
Stravinsky, Igor
Strayhorn, Billy
Streisand, Barbra
Styne, Jule
Sullivan, Ed
Summer, Donna
Szell, George
Taylor, James
Taylor, Michelle
Tchaikovsky, Piotr
    Ilyich
Thomas, Carla
Thomas, Irma
Thomas, Rufus
Thompson, Virgil
Tolstoy, Leo
Toscanini, Arturo
Tripp, Paul
Turner, Joe
Turner, Tina
Tyner, McCoy
Vache, Warren
Vaughan, Sarah

Verdi, Giuseppe
Wagner, Richard
Waits, Tom
Walker, T-Bone
Waller, Fats
Walter, Bruno
Walton, Cedar
Warner, Sylvia
    Townsend
Washington, Grover,
    Jr.
Washington, Kenny
Watts, Charlie
Wess, Frank
West, Paula
Whalum, Kurt
Whiteman, Paul
Wilde, Oscar
Wilson, Gerald
Wilson, Nancy
Wolf, Hugo
Wonder, Stevie
Woode, James
    "Jimmy"
Woods, Phil
Wordsworth, William
Young, Lester
Zappa, Frank
Zawinul, Joe
Zorn, John